An
Assemblage
of
Indian Army
Soldiers & Uniforms

'There is no man who has a higher opinion, or ought to have a higher opinion, of the sepoys than I have. I have tried them on many serious occasions, and they have never failed me, and always conducted themselves well.'

Major General Sir Arthur Wellesley
(later 1st Duke of Wellington) 1805

An Assemblage of

Indian Army Soldiers
& Uniforms

from the original paintings
by the late
CHATER PAUL CHATER

written and edited by
Michael Glover

Foreword by Antony Brett-James

LONDON
PERPETUA PRESS
1973

First Edition published November 1973
by
Perpetua Press 11 Kendall Place London W1

Filmset in 'Monophoto' Apollo by
BAS Printers Limited Wallop Hampshire
Printed in five colours
on a special making of Conqueror
Vellum Laid manufactured at Wiggins Teape's Dover
Mill by Drukkerij De Lange/Van Leer BV in the
Netherlands
Layout: Robin Ellis Cartographer: William Bromage
Bound in Winchester Buckram by Robert Hartnoll
Bodmin Cornwall

Contents

1st (Prince Albert Victor's Own) Punjab Cavalry. 1900.

The examples of Chater's studies for heads which have been inserted in the text are not necessarily correct in every detail. Some of them are incomplete and some seem to have been abandoned when the artist realised that a detail was wrong. None of them were titled by Chater and the titles given them are in some cases very tentative. They have however great interest as showing how the artist worked.

List of Plates

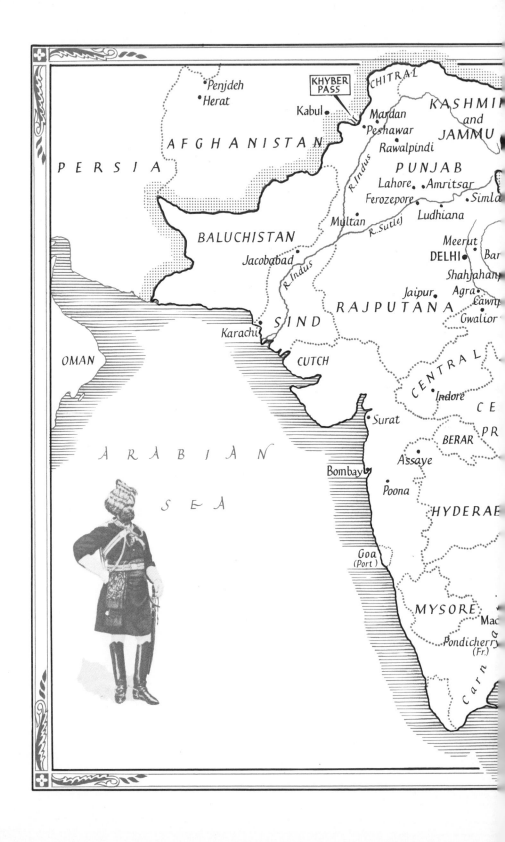

KHYBER
PASS

•Penjdeh
•Herat

CHITRAL

KASHMIR
and
JAMMU

Kabul•

Mardan•
•Peshawar

Rawalpindi•

AFGHANISTAN

PERSIA

PUNJAB

R. Indus

Lahore• •Amritsar

Ferozepore• •Simla

Ludhiana•

BALUCHISTAN

Multan• R. Sutlej

Meerut•
DELHI• Bar

Jacobabad•

R. Indus

Shahjahan

Jaipur• Agra• Cawn

RAJPUTANA

Gwalior•

OMAN

SIND

Karachi•

CUTCH

CENTRAL

Indore•

CE
PR

Surat•

BERAR

ARABIAN

Assaye•

Bombay•

SEA

Poona•

HYDERA

Goa
(Port)

MYSORE

Mad

Pondicherry
(Fr.)

Carn

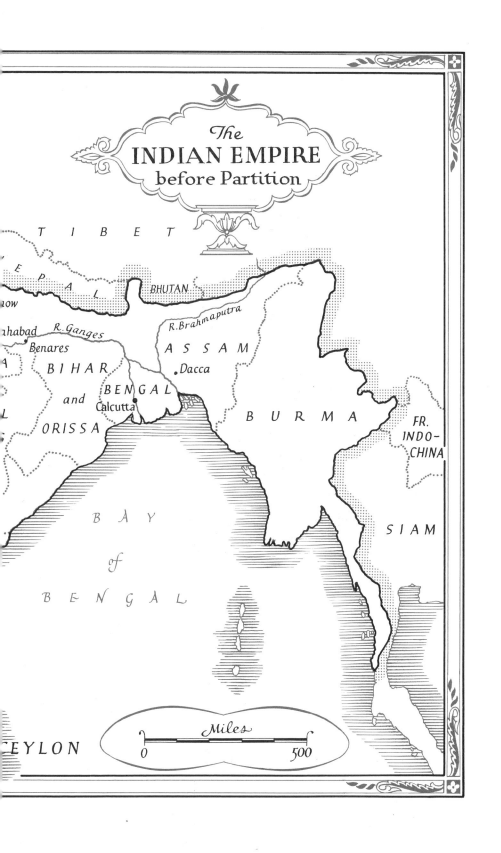

The
INDIAN EMPIRE
before Partition

TIBET

NEPAL

BHUTAN

ow

ahabad R.Ganges

Benares

R.Brahmaputra

BIHAR

ASSAM

•Dacca

BENGAL

and

Calcutta

ORISSA

BURMA

FR.
INDO-
CHINA

BAY

of

BENGAL

SIAM

Miles

0   500

CEYLON

15th Lancers, 1937.

Foreword

The old Indian Army, which was divided in 1947 after close on two hundred years, was a great body of volunteers, largely composed of soldiers who for generations followed each other, son to father, nephew to uncle, in the same regiments and corps. One reason for this continuity was pride in the profession of arms. A soldier could be proud of his calling; his prestige stood high – in Muslim eyes the warrior ranks first, for Hindus he stands second only to the priest – and when he returned to his village on either leave or retirement he was received with respect. Additional factors were at work to impel young men to enlist in the army: pressures from leaders in the village; the reliance of numerous families on the savings sent home by soldier sons; and recruiting visits by British officers to the districts whence a particular regiment drew its men.

Such officers were normally welcomed as friends, almost as relations. Despite the fact that officers and men had such different religious beliefs and personal habits, the relationship between the two, based as it was upon trust and affection, could survive the hardest tests in peace and war. Indeed it drew strength from shared discomfort, deprivation and danger. When, on rare occasions, the Indian soldier lost confidence in his officers, trouble could ensue, but otherwise the loyalty of the jawan went far beyond that to be found in most other armies, was heart-warming, and spurred on his officers to their finest efforts.

What variety in the types of soldiers who served in the army of the Queen Empress or King Emperor! Rajputs, Mahrattas, Punjabi Mussulmans, Sikhs, Jats, Ranghars, Pathans, Dogras, Baluchis, Garwalis, Madrassis from the south, and, of course, Gurkhas from Nepal. Many infantry battalions and regiments of cavalry were of mixed composition, men of different religions being organized into separate companies and squadrons. Some believed in Mahomet and turned daily towards Mecca to pray and prostrate themselves on tiny mats. Others made sacrifices to many Hindu gods. Brahma, the creator of all things, Vishnu the preserver and Siva the destroyer of life. They might worship the monkey god, Hanuman; Lakshmi, the goddess of prosperity; Ganesh, the merchant's god with his fat body and elephant's head; and Krishna, the flute-player and god of joy. A minority, mostly from Madras, belonged to the Christian Church.

Some of the troops ate rice, others ate wheat. While many liked meat, no Muslim would defile himself by taking pork, and beef was taboo to a Hindu. Not a few were vegetarians. At home they might speak one out of several dozen languages, among them Punjabi, Pushtu, Mahratti, Telegu, Tamil and Malayalam, but within the army they learnt and spoke the *lingua franca*, Hindustani.

Whereas Sikhs, for instance, were proud and physically impressive, others, such as Mahrattas or Dogras, appeared at first sight to be the very reverse; yet they were soldiers to be relied on and admired, being tenacious, long-enduring and very brave. Some belonged to the warrior classes which long ago had opposed the Muslim invasion of India, others had been among Britain's most doughty opponents in the nineteenth century, while others again had shorter traditions, dating their early battle honours to the First World War.

Before enlistment most of them had seen but little of their immense country. Self-contained and restricted had been their existence. Contacts with the outside world, with the world beyond the nearest town, had been rare. Burdened by taxation and debts, often obliged to contract new debts with powerful money-lenders, most of the soldiers had been small yeoman farmers, who tended their plot of land with the help of buffalo and ox, struggling to eke out a living in the face of drought and flood, storms of hail or sand, and damage to their crops from locusts and such-like pests.

While on service either within the confines of the Indian sub-continent or, in the present century, beyond the seas, the soldiers would think back to evenings spent smoking the hookah, and often indulged this pastime in the regiment. To their ears came the hum of the spinning-wheel, the beating of drums at some Hindu festival, the crackle of a fire that fed on cakes of dried cow dung. Their nostrils might twitch to recall the mingled smell of sandalwood and sunbaked mud walls, or of thatched roofs blackened by smoke. Now it was the greasy, rancid aroma of *ghi*, now the scent of sweetmeat stalls in the local bazaar. In memory's eye flitted scenes from an Indian village half hidden among palm or banyan trees; scenes of the village pond to which their women, moving barefoot, arms and right shoulder bare, wearing bright clothes, brass anklets and glass bangles, carried jars on their heads, did the laundry and chattered while filling the jars; and scenes of older men clad only in loincloth and turban, guiding the plough, and of naked children running along dusty tracks just as they themselves had run not so many years before. The silence was broken not only by lively voices but by the creaking of irrigation wheels in some districts and always by the creaking of carts which, drawn by two bullocks and laden with sacks of grain or with raw sugar or straw, lumbered slowly on wooden wheels in the heat.

It is of these soldiers that Paul Chater made his paintings, it is of this splendid army that Michael Glover has traced the history and changing role on the one hand and, on the other, commented on the uniforms, analyzing the interaction of four factors: Economy, Impressiveness, Recognizability, Utility; and showing the tug between the simplification imposed by active service and the elaboration imposed by ceremonial duties and the routine of peaceful soldiering.

One could scarcely disagree with Mr Glover that Chater painted with exceptional skill, beauty and accuracy. That he did so without having served in the Indian Army of his day or having lived in India after the age of twenty makes his achievement all the more remarkable. His rare ability to paint with equal talent uniforms and the men who wore them is the more surprising when one recalls that Chater had no training in art and probably never painted from a live model, basing his pictures instead on photographs and dress regulations. It is a matter of real regret that so many of the paintings appear to have been given away by the artist, or 'lost'. Yet those that have survived and which Mr Glover, who spent many years in the British Army as an officer in the Sherwood Foresters and served alongside Indian troops during the Italian campaign, rightly describes as an 'assemblage' bear witness to a painter's craftsmanship and understanding and to some at least of those very likeable and excellent soldiers with whom it was a privilege for their officers to work.

ANTONY BRETT-JAMES
July 1973

1st Bengal Cavalry. 1890.

12th Bengal Cavalry. 1890.

Introduction

This book is called an 'assemblage' of Indian Army soldiers and uniforms and it sets out to be no more than that. Anyone wanting detailed information on the style and development of the uniform of the armies of British India should turn to W. Y. Carman's two admirable volumes on 'Indian Army Uniforms' published in 1961 and 1969. Those who wish to master the involuted genealogy of the Indian regiments must consult five articles by the Marquess of Cambridge published in the *Journal of the Society for Army Historical Research* in 1969–70. Anyone who wants a comprehensive history of the Indian Army, a work comparable to that which Sir John Fortescue did for the British Army, will have to write it himself. It is to be hoped that before some British government decides to disperse the mass of material in the old India Office Library someone will undertake to fill this glaring gap in British and Indian military history.

This assemblage is based on a collection of watercolours by Chater Paul Chater, an amateur artist who is, to all intents and purposes, unknown. The paintings on which the plates are based are in the possession of Mr Ken Brickwood, Chater's son-in-law. They represent only a small proportion of the artist's output. About a hundred more were 'lost' in Cyprus in 1964. Although the whole of Chater's Indian paintings did not represent a comprehensive collection of the army's uniforms, his inveterate habit of giving them away, frequently to casual acquaintances, would have militated against publishing a complete collection. Also missing are his working drawings. To judge by a number of preliminary sketches for the uniforms of the Scottish regiments which have been preserved, they would have been of exceptional interest. As it stands it is a miscellaneous collection but one painted with remarkable skill and beauty.

Similarly the text is an assemblage. It would be inappropriate to encapsulate these plates in an academic or comprehensive study of the armies that the British raised in India. On the other hand some background is necessary if the pictures are to be regarded as anything but examples of intricate and exquisite handiwork. Despite appearances, especially among Indian examples, uniforms are not designed as works of art.

All uniforms start as functional clothing although, notably among the Household troops of all nations, the original function was to impress the beholder with the grandeur and glory of their master. As time goes on uniforms are modified. Features designed to perform new functions are introduced. Features whose function has fallen into disuse are sometimes discarded. Sometimes they are retained as one of the details that go to make up the body of regimental tradition, as with the Oxfordshire and Buckinghamshire Light Infantry (43rd/52nd) who retained their gorget patches for more than a century after the wearing of the gorget was discontinued. They were an anachronism but they did no harm to anyone else and meant a lot to the officers who wore them and to the men they commanded.

A sword-belt clearly remains a functional feature as long as swords are worn; it remains functional even if it is decked with gold lace and backed with red morocco while the sword it supports is used only for saluting. On the other hand there is the shoulder-belt worn by cavalry officers. Its origins were strictly functional. At the back was a pouch large enough to accommodate several useful accessories. One British regiment were instructed to keep their pistols in their pouches. At the lowest part of the belt was a swivel from which a carbine could be hung. In the centre of the chest was a regimental device for recognition purposes and round it was a chain that secured pickers for clearing the touch-holes of flintlock (or even matchlock) pistols.

Over the years all these functions vanished. By about 1860 pistols no longer had touch-holes that needed clearing. Some regiments retained their pickers. Others replaced them with whistles, but whistles are for active service and very soon shoulder-belts ceased to be worn on active service. The swivel was discontinued because the later type of carbine had to be carried in a leather 'bucket' attached to the saddle. The regimental device had never been of much use for recognition; it became less so in the Indian Army where so many regiments adopted a badge of crossed lances and a numeral that even the keen-sighted could not distinguish between one badge and another at more than six paces. Some regiments added their battle honours to the belt. This helped to build *esprit de corps* among the members of the regiment, who knew what the honours were. They conveyed little to a stranger who could not tell the difference between *Assaye* and *Tel-el-Kebir* at a range of more than a few feet.

The shoulder-belt obstinately survived. Some regiments swept away all ornamentation, as in the 4th Bengal Cavalry, and it became a matter of pride that their officers wore belts in plain gold lace whereas others cluttered theirs up with gilt or silver knick-knacks. The only remaining functional feature of the belt was the pouch, but this had been reduced to such a small size that it could not accommodate anything larger than two boxes of matches – and these were inaccessible to the wearer. The elaborate embroidery made it almost impossible to open even when it was not situated between the shoulder-blades.

One of the objects of the text, therefore, is to indicate the background against which the uniforms were evolved and worn, both in the Indian setting and in terms of the factors that affect the design of military clothing all over the world. The text has deliberately been kept anecdotal and fragmentary. It could be described as an entertainment with informative overtones. In particular little reference is made to the fighting record of the Indian Army. Since the author fought next door to the 4th Indian Division at Gemmano in the Gothic line in Italy, it can be assumed that he does not underestimate their prowess.

The book deals only with the period up to 1914 and the term Indian Army will henceforward be used in the sense that it then bore: the British-led force raised in what is now India, Pakistan and Bangladesh. Similarly, India should be taken to mean the whole subcontinent including Burma, but not Ceylon which, by some quirk of British policy, never came under the government in Calcutta or Delhi. Even within this area no reference is made to the forces of the princely states known as Imperial Service Troops.

In the spelling of proper names I have tried to follow the forms that were usual in Britain before independence. Few British readers would have difficulty in realizing that the Khaiber is what they think of as the Khyber Pass but Lacknau and Khanpur are less easy to identify than Lucknow and Cawnpore. In the names of regiments I have tried to follow the spellings used in their official titles. There are difficulties and inconsistencies in doing this and it is, for example, hard to pin down the precise moment when Balooch became Baluch. In this case I have used Baluch throughout. In the same way the Scinde Horse seems to have spelled itself thus from the beginning, although the spellings Sind or Sindh appear to have been more common at most times in both English and Indian usage. It is certain, however, that whether or not Sir Charles Napier made his famous pun '*Peccavi*' (and the odds are that he did not), he believed that he had conquered Scinde.

Chater Paul Chater was born in Calcutta of British parents in 1879.

11th (Prince of Wales's Own)
Bengal Lancers, 1893.

He lived in India for about twenty years before coming to England to study mining engineering. He did not complete the course. It was fortunate that he did not have to earn his living as it seems that he would not have been very good at doing so. He spent some time in the Far East as assistant to his uncle, Sir Paul Chater, one of the great Hong Kong merchants. He was not cut out for a business career and his value to the firm was more social than commercial. He travelled widely in the East and married Miss Aileen Balthazar, daughter of another great eastern trading house. They had one daughter, who became Mrs Brickwood in 1940 and died twelve years later.

Chater was a member of the Hong Kong and Shanghai Volunteer Defence Force but when war broke out in 1914 he returned to Britain and was commissioned in the Cameronians (Scottish Rifles), with whom he served, except for a period of secondment to the King's Own Scottish Borderers, until the end of the war. He fought in France and Gallipoli and was demobilized after the Armistice as a captain.

After the war he settled in London but both he and his wife were used to the Far East and they found the English winters cold. They started to spend them on the Riviera until in the early twenties they moved to Nice, where they lived until they returned to a flat in Kensington in 1931.

It was while he was living in Nice that Chater started to paint pictures of Indian Army uniforms. He had no training in art and his

5th Gurkha (Rifle) Regiment, 1887.

extraordinary manual dexterity was the more surprising since on the surface he was a hearty, charming, outdoor type, always gay, easy-going and exuberant. He had a plus handicap at golf and was a confirmed pub-goer. After his return to England he was a *habitué* of The Pembroke Arms in the Earls Court Road, a district not then as seedy as it has since become. It was there that he founded a private drinking circle known as 'The Mice'. The title was taken from a remark ascribed to George Graves, the comedian, that he 'was paid on Friday night and spent Saturday morning chasing pink mice with a butterfly net'. The initiates, who included an MP and an assistant editor of *The Times*, wore a tie decorated with pink mice and butterfly nets. In the middle thirties he took a flat in the West Cromwell Road and there, after The Pembroke Arms had closed, he was liable to spend the rest of the night playing *vingt-et-un* with his friends. As his eyesight began to fail he took to constructing intricate 8-inch ship models, which he found less taxing to his eyes than painting. Never happier than when attending a party, he was a cook of note and up to his death in 1949 was collecting for publication a book of Indian recipes. He was always a generous man even when the income from his eastern investments shrank to a trickle during the Second World War.

An expert on historical uniforms recently remarked that it was a tragedy that the artists who got the uniforms right always painted the wearers as if they were stuffed dummies, while those who could paint real live men always fell down on the details of the uniform. As a generalization this is depressingly true but it is certainly not applicable to Chater. However glorious and accurate the uniforms he depicted the portraits of the wearers are always fascinating. Yet it is improbable that he ever painted from a live model. Indians of the military classes were almost unprocurable on the Riviera in 1928 and they were rarer in Earls Court than they have since become. He therefore based his pictures entirely on printed material. Many were derived from published works, mostly from magazines such as the *Illustrated London News* and the *Navy and Army Illustrated*, both periodicals with a very high standard of photographic reproduction. None of them, of course, was printed in colour. Indeed colour printing in those days was as likely to mislead as to inform. The details of colour he obtained from *Indian Dress Regulations* and similar reference books, of which he acquired a fine library. He was also a regular student at the India Office Library, checking details that he could not confirm elsewhere.

According to his son-in-law he would start by making 'a rough sketch, paying particular attention to the face in order to ensure that it was correct for the particular regiment – Sikh, Dogra, Pathan, Punjabi or whatever it might be. His next move was to check all the details of colours, badges, medal ribbons against the *Dress Regulations*. Having got all the uniform details in note form on his rough sketch, the next step was to do the head on a much larger scale than the figure was to be; this was to ensure that all the detail was correct before reducing it to fit on the body in the final drawing. All the colour details and fine work on the eventual drawing had to be painted under a magnifying glass.' A few of the preliminary drawings of heads, some in more than one version, have been preserved and are reproduced in this book.

Not all the source material was in the form of photographs. There was no shortage of coloured reproductions of Indian uniforms. Chater certainly used some of these, especially the works of A. C. Lovett and Richard Simkin, as a basis, but only as a basis. Occasionally a pose was adopted from an earlier painting but every detail was cross-checked and verified. Above all the face was a genuine creation of Chater's and the figure had none of the woodenness of so much of Simkin's work.

Very occasionally apparent errors creep in. For the most part these were in the titles of regiments or in the date ascribed to a particular regiment. Such minor errors are excusable, since there was no check list to which reference could be made for more than two decades after the artist's death. In a very small number of cases there seem to be minor errors in the details of a uniform. But it must be remembered that in all British-inspired armies there is always a tendency to depart from the strict letter of the *Regulations*, either because some old garment is being 'worn out' before being replaced with a newly authorized pattern or because of some whim of regimental particularism. The fact that a few of these uniforms are not strictly according to the rules is more likely to mean that someone was wearing non-regulation dress than that Chater made a mistake.

In writing this book I have been helped with advice and information from many people. In particular I am obliged to Ken Brickwood, Chater's son-in-law. Without the assistance of Miranda Kelsey and Stephanie Glover the whole project would have been impossible and I am most grateful to both of them. My thanks are also due to Mr W. Y. Carman and Miss Daphne Edmonds of the National Army Museum, to Captain R. G. Hollies Smith of the Parker Gallery, to Lieutenant Colonel J. R. B. Nicholson and John Edgcumbe of *Tradition*, to Lieutenant Colonel T. M. O'H. Lowe, to Mr William Bromage for drawing the map of India, and the staffs of the library of the Royal United Services Institute and the London Library. Above all, I am grateful to my wife for every kind of help and comfort.

*This book is respectfully dedicated
to the memory of the late
Chater Paul Chater*

PART I

THE ARMIES OF INDIA

(1609–1914)

Chapter One

THE ARMIES OF THE HONOURABLE COMPANY

In 1608 William Hawkins landed at Surat with the 300-ton ship *Hector* chartered by the Company of Merchants of London Trading to the East Indies under a charter granted eight years earlier by Queen Elizabeth. His purpose was to establish a trading station or, as it was then called, a factory. Finding that permission to do so could be obtained only from the Mughal Emperor at Agra he set off for the capital on 1 February 1609. As escort he hired 50 Pathans, the first military force to be raised by the British in India. It was a wise precaution. On his way he was ambushed, not as might have been expected by the freebooting bands that were to be such a destructive feature of the Indian landscape for the next two and a half centuries, but by Portuguese merchants anxious to preserve their trade monopoly. The Pathans beat off the attack.

The early factories established by the East India Company – Surat in 1619, Madras in 1640, Calcutta in 1690 – were guarded by Europeans recruited for the purpose. In 1662 King Charles II received Bombay from the Portuguese on his marriage to Catherine of Braganza. He sent out as a garrison a battalion of 400 regulars under Sir Abraham Shipman but the Portuguese at Bombay had not heard of the arrangement and refused to let the troops land. They had to wait on an inhospitable island near Goa until authority arrived from Lisbon. Eventually, in 1665, Bombay was handed over, but by that time only one officer and 113 men of the king's troops survived and Mahrattas were recruited to make up the numbers. Three years later the king made Bombay over to the Company in return for a loan of £50,000 at 6 per cent and a rent of £10 a year, which was paid until 1739. The mixed regiment was transferred to the Company's service.

The task of guarding the Company's factories continued to be a task for Europeans, with a few native auxiliaries, until the middle of the eighteenth century. The turning-point came in 1746, when Madras was captured by the French with 1,100 Europeans and 400 drilled Indians. This little army next attempted to take another

British factory, Fort David, south of Pondicherry, but it was frustrated by the landing of 100 regulars and a number of seamen and marines. These, apart from King Charles's levy, were the first British servicemen to serve in India. Next year more regulars, 12 independent companies and 800 marines, were disembarked in an attempt to take Pondicherry. They failed at a cost of 1,000 British dead. In 1754 the first complete British regiment to serve in India, the 39th Foot, were disembarked. From that date British regiments were to be stationed in India until 1947.

Meanwhile in 1746 Captain Stringer Lawrence, a regular officer who had fought at Culloden, was sent to Madras as commander of the Company's forces with the rank of major 'in the East Indies only'. He organized a European regiment in Madras and recruited and trained a large number of Indians although, following the French practice, he did not organize them into units larger than company strength. The first battalion of sepoys was raised by Robert Clive in Bengal in 1757, the year after Calcutta was captured by Siraj-ud-daulah, the Nabob of Bengal, Orissa and Bihar. The 1st Battalion, Bengal Native Infantry were the only complete Indian battalion to earn the battle honour *Plassey* in 1757.

The Honourable East India Company acquired an army in the last half of the eighteenth century. In fact they acquired three armies. Each of their three presidencies – Bengal, Madras and Bombay – had by 1770 a commander-in-chief, a small European contingent raised and paid for by the Company, and a large native force comprising cavalry, artillery and infantry. At the beginning of the nineteenth century there were in Bengal 8 regiments of cavalry (including a bodyguard) and 43 battalions of infantry. The Madras Army, with 8 regiments and 40 battalions, was almost as large. In Bombay there were only 19 battalions. In addition the Company rented from the home government a substantial number of British regular regiments and battalions. Even without them they were maintaining an army as large as most European powers and could also count on contingents furnished by native rulers allied or feudatory to the Council. Unfortunately both the largest army and the supreme commander, who, like the governor general, was appointed by the British government after 1773, were stationed in Bengal, the Indian centre furthest from Britain, weeks of sailing time further than either of the other presidency capitals. This was due to the fact that the British possessions in Madras and Bombay were very small in area, while in Bengal the Company already owned substantial tracts of territory. This was unfortunate, since Bengal produced recruits who compared unfavourably with other parts of the subcontinent and who posed greater administrative problems on religious grounds.

King George III remarked that a trading company had no business to have an army and it would be hard to disagree with him. (The situation became even more unusual after 1833 when the HEIC ceased trading altogether.) To do them justice the Company would gladly have dispensed with the doubtful and expensive privilege of maintaining so large a force. In their view they had no option. They had gone to India to trade and for more than a century they had done no more than provide guards for their establishments. After about 1740 the situation changed completely. On the one hand the French were determined to disrupt British trade in India and could deploy many more troops, European and Indian, than the Company could muster to achieve this end. On the other hand conditions in India were changing. Akbar, the greatest of the Mughal emperors, died a few years before William Hawkins reached Surat. From the reign of his son onwards the power of the Muslim Mughals was progressively sapped by a race of Hindu horsemen, the Mahrattas. Before the end of the eighteenth century they had established themselves in a vast tract of land in central India. The Mahratta Confederation reached the sea on either coast; it stretched as far south as the borders of Mysore, beyond Delhi to the north. The Mughal emperor, in whose name the Mahratta princes claimed to rule, was a prisoner in his palace.

There was no unity of policy or purpose within the Confederation. There were five principal rulers and a host of minor chieftains who indulged in constant warfare among themselves. Only a powerful external threat, usually from the north-west, could produce a temporary, fragile unity among them.

The Mahrattas did not excel at the business of government. To them it began and ended with the collection of the land revenue. Since the repeated passage of ill-disciplined armies in the endemic civil wars ruined agriculture it became increasingly difficult to collect the revenue and tax-gathering became itself an operation of war. It became necessary to use troops to extort revenue and the troops seldom stopped at collecting what was strictly due. Worse, because less predictable, than the actions of the rulers were the depredations of gangs of disbanded soldiery who owed allegiance to no one and were concerned solely with loot. Many of these were not Mahrattas but soldiers of fortune from all over India and beyond, Pathans being particularly prominent. Such predatory bands made peace more hideous for the peasant than war. Thomas Munro, one of the Company's most distinguished civil servants (who could also turn his hand to soldiering), described what happened to the district of Cuddapore when peace broke out in 1801:

> A mutinous unpaid army was turned loose during the sowing season to collect their pay from the villages. They drove off and sold the cattle, extorted money by torture from every man who fell into their hands, and plundered the houses and shops of those who fled.

All India outside the parts controlled, directly or indirectly, by the Company became a paradise for the freebooter. George Thomas, an illiterate Irish sailor, succeeded by force of personality in establishing himself as Rajah of Hariana. Everywhere there was extortion and looting. In the process India was well on the way to becoming a desert. A report prepared in 1817 showed that in Indore 1,663 villages out of a total of 3,701 were deserted and that in the district of Dhar only 46 out of 351 villages were still inhabited. It was hardly to be expected that acts of violence would stop short at the boundaries of the Company's territory or at those of the rulers who allied themselves to the Company.

The Company never doubted that they had the right and duty to defend their own territory and seldom deserted their Indian allies. There was disagreement about what they should do in the rest of India. The straightforward question of how to stop raids into friendly territory developed into a moral problem. Two schools of thought developed. One side believed that the native states should be left to sort out their own problems in their own bloody way. Against them were those who maintained that it was the duty of the British to impose peace and prosperity on the warring factions.

The arguments between the quietists and the expansionists raged for a century. British policy swung from one extreme to the other but gradually the expansionists prevailed. By 1850 the whole sub-continent was either under the Company's control or under the rule of an Indian prince in close alliance with the Company. There was no conscious imperialism – that did not emerge until the second half of the century. Even the expansionists had no ambition to acquire territory as such. Trade, the original purpose of the British presence in India, played a declining part in the thinking behind the expansion. Britain conquered her Indian Empire without deliberate design. She had set out to trade; then she had determined not to let the chaos that was India fall under the influence of any other European power. By 1811, when the French menace had been finally disposed of, the

Company found themselves saddled, most unwillingly, with a civilizing mission that took up so much of the Company's time that trading had to be abandoned.

Although many of the Company's servants in the eighteenth century behaved disgracefully and the wealth of retiring 'nabobs' was a constant scandal in Britain in the days of the younger Pitt (whose great-grandfather had been a conspicuous 'nabob'), the senior officials in India embraced the civilizing mission at quite an early stage. In 1768 the Governor of Bengal instructed his 'district officers':

> Among the chief effects which are hoped from your residence in that province are to convince the ryot [peasant] that you will stand between him and the hand of oppression; that you will be his refuge and the redresser of his wrongs; that honest and direct application to you will never fail producing speedy and equitable decisions; that, after supplying the legal due of the government, he may be secure in the enjoyment of the remainder.

Whatever else the British did in India she gave the peasant peace and security such as he had not known for centuries. Disputes about the morality of the British conquest of India will continue indefinitely but, on a practical level, it is difficult to disagree with Charles Napier's verdict on the conquest of Sind. It was 'a very advantageous, useful, humane piece of rascality'.

To maintain the usefulness and the humanity the Company needed an army. To supply it with officers they established in 1810 a college at Addiscombe, near Croydon; this was to be the military equivalent of Haileybury, where they trained their civil servants. The military training was entirely theoretical but it was in many ways an advance on the practice of the royal army. The Crown had had a Military Academy for officers of the engineers and the artillery since 1741. Since 1792 the Company had been entitled to send to Woolwich up to 40 cadets at a time at a charge of £100 a year. For the cavalry and infantry the British arrangements were very sketchy. The Royal Military Academy had been established in 1802 but it could accommodate only 120 cadets, 20 of whom were the Company's nominees at 90 guineas a year. Up to the time of Waterloo only one newly commissioned officer in 25 for the royal army had passed through the College. The Company were more thorough. Almost all their potential officers were expected to pass through Addiscombe. Those who passed the course at the top of the list were commissioned into the engineers, the next batch went to the artillery and the remainder to the infantry. Commissions to the cavalry regiments were in the gift of the directors of the Company, no training being considered necessary.

It was no light matter to accept a commission in the Company's army. Lord Roberts, who became a second lieutenant in the Bengal artillery in 1851, wrote that:

> under the regulations then in force, leave, except on medical certificate, could only be obtained once during the officer's service and ten years had to be spent in India before that leave could be taken.

India was notoriously an unhealthy climate and the death rate from disease was high. The newly commissioned officer would be assailed by a barrage of forbidding advertisements from the insurance companies offering 'special rates on the lives of Military Officers proceeding to or residing in India'. One company went so far as to include this class of business under the heading 'Invalid Lives'. The dangers involved in getting to India were underlined by an advertisement in the *Army List* for travelling trunks:

> . . . so constructed that they are perfectly air and water tight: and when packed with apparel will float on the water with such buoyancy that they will preserve from sinking as many persons as can attach themselves to them; and a trunk of ordinary dimensions will sustain in the water from six to eight grown persons who can easily get a secure hold by means of a lashing, with loops appended to it, which is applied instantaneously. In many cases of shipwreck these trunks would be invaluable: affording to the owner a SECURE BUOY by which he may float to shore or ride safely on the surface of the water till assistance comes.

Assuming that he avoided shipwreck the officer could look forward to a long and tedious voyage. Under sail it could take ten months to reach Calcutta. Roberts went out, mostly by steamer, in 1852. He took forty-one days. This included a 90-mile journey through the desert later crossed by the Suez Canal. This was accomplished in a vehicle for six passengers drawn by mules and 'closely resembling a bathing machine'. Reaching Calcutta was only a start. Roberts had to travel from the artillery depot at Dum Dum, just outside the capital, to his battery at Peshawar. Travelling alone it took him three months to make the journey. It would have taken him much longer if he had had to move with troops. When not marching, officers went by cart. In the same decade another officer described the pleasures of travelling in:

. . . a very strong wooden cart, on two wheels, without the faintest attempt at springs, and with a fragile roof . . . this primitive conveyance, being drawn by two bullocks and driven by a native, and travelling at a brisk two to two and a half miles per hour! Each bullock-train consists of large numbers of these carriages, from twenty-five to forty generally, . . . travelling during the night, and halting during the heat of the day at appointed stations, which one ordinarily arrives at about eight A.M. or nine A.M., and leaving again about three o'clock in the afternoon. Temporary sheds have been erected for the men at these halting-places, while there is generally a 'dak-bungalow' (post-house) for the accommodation of the officers.

The Company modelled its army, in drill, discipline and dress, on the royal army. Although there were commissioned Indians there was a very high proportion of British officers, 24 to each battalion. Often these officers slavishly copied the less reputable of their regular colleagues. As early as 1810 one of the Company's Madras Engineers said:

> There was a too evident desire to copy the European regiments in matters not really essential to the discipline of the native corps but, at the same time, tending to produce discontent and diminish their attachment to the service. For instance, the frequent drills, parades and roll-calls, though absolutely necessary to preserve the Europeans, whose habits are anything but temperate or quiescent, in any degree of order, were by no means so to the sober and domestic sepoy who, fond of his ease, becomes discontented by unnecessary duty.

The Company's failure to realize the differences between their British and Indian soldiers was, particularly in Bengal, to prove disastrous. Conditions in the British Army were such that only 'the scum of the earth' would join it. Tours of duty were long even in the royal army and even when they came to an end men were encouraged to transfer to incoming units to make up the numbers. In the Company's European regiments the recruit signed on for a lifetime of service in India. As long as there were active operations 'the scum of the earth', in royal or Company service, showed up well and were reasonably healthy. Deterioration set in sharply in the increasingly long periods of inactivity. The conditions under which the soldiers lived did everything to encourage the disease that was in any case rife in India. When Florence Nightingale investigated the health of the army in India she found that the annual death rate was 69 per 1,000:

'A company out of every regiment has been sacrificed every twenty months.' Much of this was due to lack of elementary sanitary precautions and unsuitable diet. Almost as much was due to drink. The soldiers were confined to barracks in the nine hottest hours of every day and they had nothing to do except drink local spirits in the canteen. Miss Nightingale acidly remarked that a cantonment was officially described as temperate if only a third of the cases admitted to hospital were suffering from the effects of alcohol.

The sepoys and sowars were of a very different type. Soldiering was regarded as an honourable profession in India and one of the problems of, particularly, the Bengal army was that the men in the ranks refused to undertake the menial tasks that British soldiers regarded as his inevitable lot. The nearest English equivalent of the type of recruit to the ranks in India would be the sons of yeomen farmers. It is significant that, with rare exceptions, the Indian cavalry regiments were raised on the *silladar* system. Under this the recruit had to provide his own horse. He would receive compensation for it if it was killed in action but, although it was fed at official expense, he would have to replace it if it died or became unfit for service through age or neglect. This system continued until the First World War, when it foundered on practical difficulties; but even subsequently the recruit had to pay a deposit on his government-issue horse, which was repaid to him when he drew his pension. This presupposed a very different type of soldier from those who enlisted in the European regiments; he was set further apart from them by the fact that, be he Hindu or Muslim, his religion forbade him the consolations of drink.

The Company's Indian regiments were not well officered. Addiscombe produced a number of officers who could stand comparison with, and frequently excel, their contemporaries in the royal army. These were men who wanted to serve in India because of a desire for adventure and a sense of high purpose, as opposed to their colleagues who joined the Company's army *faute de mieux*. Such men were not content to suffer the stultifying routine of peacetime cantonments. They obtained extra-regimental appointments where their talents could be, and were, put to good use.

It is invidious to single out one of the Company's officers to serve as an example of the heights they could achieve, for the list is long and their exploits remarkable by any standard. But from such names as Harry Lumsden, Robert Napier, John Nicholson, James Outram and Frederick Roberts it is possible to pick John Jacob, if only because his family continued to give outstanding service, for the most part in India, from John Jacob himself down to the present representative, a lieutenant general who has not only commanded troops on the frontier and served as Assistant Military Secretary to Churchill's war cabinet but crowned his career as Director General of the BBC. Versatility was always the most outstanding characteristic of the best British officers in India.

John Jacob was the son of a Wiltshire vicar and went to India from Addiscombe in 1828 as an officer of Bombay artillery at the age of sixteen. As soon as he had a chance to go on active service he showed a genius for raising and leading irregular troops. His first campaign was at the head of an improvised battery of artillery. In the middle of it he showed his talent as an engineer. When the force to which he was attached was held up by a 'sheep-walk' through a narrow gorge he formed a scratch battalion of sappers from a handful of pioneers and a horde of camp-followers and had a track passable for all arms within four days.

Although he had been a stammerer from birth he trained and led the two regiments of Scinde Irregular Horse* until, in his own opinion and in that of all who saw them, they were 'equal to the best Europeans. Though called Irregular Horse, we are as regular as Her Majesty's Life Guards.' The irregularity lay in the fact that they were trained and armed according to Jacob's own ideas and had only 6 British officers to 1,600 men. Both in Jacob's Horse and in the two infantry regiments he raised (1st and 2nd Baluch Rifles) all promotion went by merit and considerations of caste were not permitted to affect any work that the soldiers had to do. Discipline was maintained almost wholly by the threat to expel a man from the regiment.

If his military exploits were remarkable they were no more so than those he performed in his civilian capacity. He took over command of the Scinde Horse in 1842 when he was still only a lieutenant.† At the same time he was given the civil government of Eastern Cutchee. Five years later he was made Political Commissioner of Upper Scinde. When he first went there Scinde was a torrid desert overrun with Baluchi robbers. First he pacified it; next he irrigated it; then he opened up communications. He constructed 2,600 miles of road, 'furnished with 786 masonry bridges, 88 of which, across navigable canals, were passable by boats of the largest size'. His memorial is the little desert town of Khangur, which was the centre of his government. Here he

---

* The Scinde Horse became known as Jacob's Horse but they were raised not by Jacob but by Lieutenant Clarke.

† He became captain by brevet in the following year. At his death in 1858 he was a regimental captain, brevet lieutenant colonel and local brigadier general.

established a flourishing town with tree-lined avenues in the centre of a fertile area which by 1855 was 5 miles wide and 20 miles long. The whole was watered by a 60-mile canal which he designed and built from the Indus river. The erstwhile robbers had become farmers – if they had failed to get into one of his regiments. Khangur was renamed Jacobabad in 1851.

In his spare time he was a superb gunsmith, designing a rifle that was accurate at 3,000 yards at a time when the British Army was issued with one that was sighted only to 1,000 yards and was of dubious accuracy at even shorter ranges. He also found time to write a work of heterodox theology.

The Company's officers who stayed to serve with their regiments were not a bit like John Jacob. The vast majority of them were second rate and conscious of the fact. Promotion was entirely by seniority and grindingly slow. There was little for them to do and no incentive for them to do it.

It is scarcely surprising that unrest was endemic in the armies of Bengal and Madras. In Bengal alone three regiments were disbanded for mutiny between 1840 and 1850. If the first reactions to the great outbreak of 1857 were sluggish it was because those in charge were old men who thought they had seen it all before.

At the end of the Sikh wars in the 1840s the Company acquired a fourth army, the Punjab Irregular Force (PIF), though it was not until 1886 that the PIF (by that time known as the Punjab Frontier Force) became a part of the Indian army. These 6 regiments of cavalry and later 11 of infantry were subject not to the commander-in-chief but to the commissioner in the Punjab. Their formation marks a shift in recruitment for all the armies. Previously the bulk of the troops had been drawn from the plains of the Ganges and the Carnatic. Henceforward the main source of recruits was to be the north-west – from Dogras, Jats, Pathans, Rajputs and Sikhs.

The PIF were never far away from active service. In the short space between the raising of the force and the outbreak of the Mutiny they evolved a breed of soldier who was to be the model for the rest of the armies when they came to be reformed. (There were some parts of the Presidency armies, notably in Bombay and in the Gurkha regiments, that needed no such model.) Since, uniquely, they comprised both cavalry and infantry the Guides can serve as an example for the whole force. When Henry Lawrence was established as Resident in the still independent Sikh kingdom, he had no troops available except a few companies of Bengal infantry to protect the Residency. Feeling the need for some mobile force he instructed Harry Lumsden to raise a small corps of Guides at Peshawar. Significantly Lumsden, a lieutenant of the 59th Bengal Native Infantry, was serving away from his regiment. He was twenty-five years old.

The Guides were raised, in the words of his second-in-command, 'unshackled by a bank and unaided by government advance'. The necessary funds were raised by stoppages of pay of those who wished to join. Lumsden required men 'accustomed to look after themselves and not easily taken aback by any sudden emergency'. They were forthcoming in almost embarrassing numbers. There were cases where men offered as much as 300 rupees to be allowed to join. Though the establishment was soon increased to one regiment of cavalry and one of infantry there were often as many as 30 would-be recruits serving with the Guides, drawing no pay while they waited for a place to fall vacant.

Technically the Guides were an 'irregular' unit. Apart from the fact of their having very few British officers, this implied that they administered themselves in a way that was effective but anathema to office-bound paymasters. There was nothing irregular about their training. Although they were expected to work independently as scouts and gatherers of information, they could mount a set-piece attack as well as any 'regular' unit. Their foot-drill they learned from instructors from the 60th Rifles and it was impeccable. The men who joined the Guides were mercenaries in the best sense of the word – professionals. Many of them came from beyond the boundaries of India, from Afghanistan, from Nepal, from Persia, from Turkestan. They were not impelled by patriotism but by pride in their chosen profession and by loyalty to their regiment. Needless to say they were superlatively officered.

Recruitment was sometimes an irregular business. One of the earliest tasks of the Guides was to hunt down a notorious bandit called Dilawur Khan. As far as he acknowledged any nationality, he was an Afghan. He had a price of 2,000 rupees on his head. Lumsden was so impressed by the skill with which he avoided capture that he sent him an invitation to visit his tent and a safe conduct. Dilawur unhesitatingly accepted and presented himself at the Guides' camp. He was astonished when Lumsden offered him a vacancy in the regiment. He asked for time to think it over. Six weeks later he reappeared, offering to enlist with as many of his band as could be found places. He made only one condition. Having been a successful commander on his own account, he felt it beneath his dignity to do recruit drill. He particularly resented the pace-step of the slow march. Lumsden pointed out to him that the slow march was an essential part of cere-monial drill, without which it would be impossible to pay due honour to any visiting 'Lord Sahib'. He, Lumsden, even did the pace-step himself on occasions. Dilawur enlisted without further argument. By 1869 he was a subadar and while on an intelligence mission fell into the hands of the Mehtar of Chitral, who imprisoned him for some time. Eventually he was released but on his way back to Peshawar he was caught in the snow on the mountain passes. As he was dying, he charged his companions: 'Should any of you reach India alive, go to the Commissioner and say, "Dilawur Khan of the Guides is dead"; and say also that he died faithful to his salt and happy to give up his life in the service of the great Queen.'

Occasionally the regiment took a recruit who was not up to their standards. In the 1870s a young Afridi sepoy, worried lest he should be required to take part in a punitive expedition against his own village, deserted with two rifles. Francis Jenkins, who was in com-mand, sent for all the deserter's fellow tribesmen serving with the detachment. There were 17 of them. He told them to hand in their arms and take off their uniforms. They were not to reappear until they had recovered the lost rifles. It was two years before they presented themselves at the regimental depot at Mardan. They handed in the two rifles and asked to be re-enlisted. They did not say what had happened to the deserter.

The Guides accounted for another deserter during the Malakand expedition in 1897. When attacking troops the tribesmen encouraged themselves by beating drums and blowing horns. In one engagement this self-encouragement was augmented by a bugler sounding calls he could have learned only in the Indian Army: 'As he suddenly col-lapsed in the middle of the "officer's mess call", we concluded that a bullet had brought him to an untimely end.'

Desertion from the Guides was a very rare phenomenon. There was none when the Mutiny broke out in 1857. The regiment was one of those sent from the Punjab to reinforce the slender 'besieging' force on the Delhi ridge. They set off from Mardan, north of the Kabul river, on 13 May. They reached the ridge, 580 miles away, on 9 June. On the way they had been delayed for five days by various causes, including a minor action. They had averaged more than 27 miles a day, infantry and cavalry alike. When they arrived their commander, Captain Daly, was asked how long it would be before they were ready for action. 'In half an hour,' he replied. Although they had marched 30 miles in the morning they were in action that afternoon.

Six hundred men of the Guides marched to Delhi. During the siege they suffered 350 casualties. Their strength in British officers was killed or wounded four times over. Not a man was lost by defection or desertion. With them was a water-carrier named Juma. Again and again he took water to wounded men lying under the blazing sun under heavy fire. After the siege he was decorated by the government but his highest reward came when the men of the Guides, who did not usually care much for lowly characters like water-carriers, petitioned that he might be enlisted. He died a jemadar, much decorated in the Second Afghan War. Rudyard Kipling commemorated him as 'Gunga Din'.

The Second Afghan War was the high-point in the history of the Guides. The Amir of Afghanistan had agreed to accept a British Resident at Kabul. On 3 September 1879 the Residency was attacked by a mob of mutinous Afghan soldiery. The escort consisted of 77 men of the Guides under Lieutenant Walter Hamilton vc. In a hopeless position they fought throughout the day. Hamilton was killed leading a third counter-attack against some guns that were battering the gate of the Residency. The civilian staff were already dead. About a dozen of the Guides were still alive when the Afghans called to them to surrender now that their English masters were dead. Jemadar Jewand Singh replied, 'The Sahibs ordered us to defend the Residency to the last. Shall we disgrace our uniforms by disobeying them now that they are dead?' All the escort died but they are said to have killed 600 of their attackers. The Committee of Inquiry which was set up to investigate the disaster reported that 'the records of no army can show a brighter record of devoted bravery than has been shown by this small band of Guides'. The Committee did not exaggerate.

If the Guides showed the nineteenth-century Indian Army at its best, the transport service showed it at its worst. One of the ways in which the Company copied the royal army was in the economical plan that there should be no permanent transport and supply organization in peacetime. In war everything was to depend on contractors (who were sometimes officers in the Company's army) and improvisation. The two armies, however, came to contrasting solutions to the problem when they engaged in active operations. When the British Army landed in Egypt in 1801 Sir John Moore complained that they were 'without a waggon or the means of conveying an article a yard from the beach'. Two years earlier Arthur Wellesley had described the advance of the combined armies of the Company (including some royal regiments) and the Nizam of Hyderabad:

The march of these two armies was almost in the form of a square or oblong, of which the front and rear were formed of cavalry, and about two or three miles in extent. The left and right (owing to the immense space taken up in the column by field pieces drawn by bullocks) about seven or eight miles. In the middle went everything belonging to the army, and the whole space was filled. You will have some idea of what was in that space when I state to you the number of bullocks which I know were in the public service, and in the employ of *brinjarries* or grain merchants, which did not compose one half of the whole number that were with the army. There were in the department of the commissary of stores about 25,000, in that of the commissary of grain about 20,000, in that of the commissary of provisions about 5,000, in that of the camp equipage about 5,000, making in all in the service of the British grand army about 60,000 bullocks, of which 15,000 were in draught, the others carried loads. The Company's bullock department in the Nizam's army had in it about 3,000 divided among the various departments. Besides this there were with the grand army about 20,000 bullocks loaded with grain belonging to the *brinjarries* and about 8,000 loaded with gram [chick peas] for the cavalry horses. The Nizam's army had with it 25,000 bullocks loaded with grain belonging to the *brinjarries*. Besides all these, the number of elephants, camels, bullocks, carts, &c., belonging to individuals in the army, particularly that of the Nizam, was beyond calculation. I have no scruple in declaring that the number of cattle in the employment of individuals was double that in the employment of the public. You may have some idea of the thing when I tell you that when all were together, there was a multitude in motion which covered about eighteen square miles.

The quantity of transport needed to move the Indian Army did not decrease with the years. In 1842 Charles Napier led a force of 3,000 fighting men into Sind and complained, 'Oh! the baggage! It is enough to drive one mad. We have 1,500 camels with their confounded long necks, each occupying fifteen feet! Fancy those long devils in a defile! four and a quarter miles of them! Then there are the donkeys, and ponies, and led horses, and bullocks innumerable.' As late as 1897 the expedition to the Tirah required 60,000 draught animals for 44,000 soldiers.

The reason for this vast transport lay in the number of followers who had to accompany the army. An officer who fought in the Mutiny explained how the problem arose:

The sick are carried in doolies . . . each one requires six men, four to carry it and two to relieve them when necessary. . . . The proportion of doolies in war time is one to every ten men; this in a regiment one thousand strong amounts to one hundred doolies – six bearers to each, total *six hundred doolie bearers* to a single regiment! Here then is the nucleus . . . of the force of camp-followers; in addition to this is the large staff of cooks, 'bhistees', 'bildahs', 'sweepers', etc., allotted to regiments . . . which of course accompanies them in full force into the field.

The regimental hospitals, too, are augmented to an overwhelming size; to each tent is allotted a 'kulassie' or tent-man, while the cavalry and artillery swell the . . . rabble by their innumerable 'syces' and grass-cutters, who are nearly in the proportion of one of each to every horse. Throw into the scale . . . hordes of hackery-drivers, camel-drivers and 'mahouts'; add to this the bazaar establishments attached to each regiment, numbering whole legions of speculative niggers . . . each officer employs also from eight to twelve servants, and this long list is closed with the numberless *employées* in the vast train of ordnance . . . and with the functionaries, baboos, etc., nearly as numerous, belonging to the commissariat department . . . the wives and families of the above, with interlopers, milk-sellers, do-nothings, lookers-on, tag-rag and bobtail attendant upon the whole, and then you may perhaps understand how it is that the non-combatant part of the army doubles, ay, and trebles, the militant portion.

Although something was done to limit the number of followers there were still 17,500 of them when 20,000 Indian troops embarked for China in 1900.

Queen Victoria

Chapter Two

SOLDIERS OF THE QUEEN EMPRESS

The death-knell of the Company's army was tolled on 11 May 1857 when General Hewett, commanding at Meerut, 40 miles from Delhi, wrote:

> I regret to have to report that the native troops' here broke out yesterday evening in open mutiny. About 6.30 p.m. the 20th Regiment, Native Infantry, turned out with arms. They were reasoned with by their officers when they reluctantly returned to their lines, but immediately after they rushed out and began to fire. The 11th Regiment, Native Infantry, turned out with their officers who had perfect control over them, inasmuch as they persuaded them not to touch their arms till Colonel Finnis had reasoned with the mutineers, in doing which he was, I regret to say, shot dead. After which the 20th Native Infantry fired into the 11th Regiment who then desired their officers to leave them, and apparently joined the mutineers.

Trouble in the Bengal Army had been brewing for a long time. In the previous month two battalions had had to be disbanded near Calcutta and there had been an ugly scene at Barrackpur when a sepoy had shot and wounded the British adjutant and sergeant major of his battalion while calling on his comrades to 'join him to defend and die for their religion and caste'. The immediate cause of the unrest was a widely circulated story that the cartridges for the newly issued Enfield rifle were smeared with the grease of pigs and cows. Assurances had been given and, apparently, accepted that this was not the case. The trouble at Barrackpur seemed to have been composed. On 7 May the general there sent back the European troops he had summoned as a precaution, reporting: 'It is not probable that I shall again require the presence of these troops at this station.'

Meanwhile the trouble at Meerut was coming to the boil. There was no question of the soldiers there losing caste by having to bite the new cartridges. The new weapons had not been issued to the regiment that started the outbreak. The captain in temporary command of the 3rd Bengal Native Cavalry wrote on 25 April: 'We have none of the objectionable cartridges, but the men say that if they fire any kind of cartridge at present they lay themselves open to the imputation of having fired the objectionable ones.'

When ammunition was issued to the 3rd Cavalry 85 men refused to accept it. A court of inquiry heard evidence from the senior Hindu and Muslim troopers of each troop. Most of them replied: 'I know of no objection to them, but yet I have a doubt in my heart.' One Muslim trooper amplified this, saying: 'I have doubts about the cartridges. They look like the old ones but they may, for all I know, have pig's fat rubbed over them.' A court martial followed. The court consisted entirely of Indian officers. They unanimously sentenced the 85 protesters to ten years' hard labour. Two members of the court voted for the death penalty.

The ceremonial degradation of these 85 men of the 3rd Cavalry was the spark that set off the Mutiny. It has been held that if General Hewett had acted immediately and firmly with the European troops at Meerut the outbreak might have been confined. He was an old man and a natural scapegoat. By the time the British regiments had been mustered it was dark. Even had there still been enough light to deal with the 3 mutinous units, his British force was not impressive. According to the man who superseded him, Hewett had available only 'the 6th Dragoon Guards (Carabineers), half of whom were recruits unable to ride, HM 60th Rifles, about 800 strong, a troop of horse artillery, a light field battery and 200 artillery recruits who had learned nothing beyond the first principles of foot drill, being totally unacquainted with gun drill and the use of the carbine'.

Once the chance, if it existed, of containing the Meerut outbreak was lost, the Mutiny spread right across the Bengal Presidency. The government did not react with much vigour at first. Mutinies in native regiments were almost commonplace. Information reaching Calcutta was far from complete and brisk action was discouraged by a telegraph message from Cawnpore on 17 May which read: 'You will be glad to hear that telegraphic communication with Meerut has been restored: this is the best proof that things are quietening down.' Nor was the governor general's position made any easier by the fact that the commander-in-chief, a veteran of Waterloo, had taken himself off with his staff to Simla, 1,000 miles away. Between Calcutta and Delhi there were only 4 British battalions, one for every 200 miles.

As soon as the government realized the extreme seriousness of the outbreak they reacted violently. Bartle Frere, Chief Commissioner of Sind, commented:

> In some things the government shows great vigour – they pass laws
> at the rate of two or three a sitting – some are not well considered –
> some very badly concocted, but they come out 'hot and hot', and
> in the absence of harder missiles must strike terror into the insur-
> gents, if their effect be at all proportioned to the difficulty of
> understanding them. Their general drift is that anyone who
> respects any one may hang anyone else.

The suppression of the Mutiny was marked by appalling brutality
on both sides. By killing all the women and children on whom they
could lay hands, the three rebellious regiments at Meerut stored up
for themselves and their comrades a terrible retribution. The massacre
at Cawnpore served to heighten the horror. The troops who recaptured
the place were not to know that the mutinous sepoys had refused to
carry out the mass killing of women and children and that butchers
had had to be hired to do the execution. The British, and the loyal
Indians, uncertain of themselves and horrified that their former
comrades could behave in such a way, overreacted and few captured
mutineers escaped with their lives.*

Whatever the underlying causes of the Mutiny it is quite certain
that it would never have taken place had it not been for the very
unsatisfactory state of the Bengal Army. Although it was the largest
of the Company's armies it had in recent years seen the least active
service. This was largely because religious reasons prevented Bengal
regiments being sent overseas. (Occasionally volunteer Bengal regiments were sent overseas, as when 5,000 Rajputs volunteered to take
part in the Java campaign in 1811.) Aden was regularly garrisoned by
Bombay units, who had also provided an expeditionary force against
Persia in 1856. Operations in Burma were almost wholly a task for the
Madras Army, who also garrisoned the Straits Settlements. Three
Madras units had taken part in the China War of 1841. The formation
of the special force on the Punjab frontier meant that the fighting on
the North-West Frontier was no longer done by the Bengal Army,
although the Punjab was technically a part of the Bengal presidency.

Since the Sikh Wars the Bengal Army settled down to being an
army of occupation in its own country. This inactivity magnified its

---

* It was the custom to execute mutineers by blowing them from the muzzle of a canon. This
was probably more humane than the slow hanging then practised. As late as 1907 Said Bilgrami,
the first Muslim appointed to the Viceroy's Council, was asked what measures should be taken
to suppress the Punjab rebellion. He recommended blowing the ringleaders from a cannon as
that was the only way Indians would understand.

long-term deficiencies. At the siege of Multan in 1848 it had been noticed that the Bombay sepoys, despite their religious prejudices, had cheerfully taken their turn with pick and shovel, while those from Bengal considered such work beneath them. Five years before the Mutiny John Jacob, a Bombay officer, publicly indicted the Bengal Army: 'The position of the sepoy is that of a spoiled child. Humoured and indulged for years past, he looks on humouring and indulgence as his right, and when from any cause these are denied to him, he sulks and rebels. Nay, he sulks and rebels even on suspicion.' Whereas in the Bombay Army Indian officers were commissioned on merit, in Bengal only length of service counted and 'if a man keeps clear of actual crime and lives long enough, he becomes a commissioned officer, however unfit'. Naturally this state of affairs rebounded on the British officers and it has been calculated that only 3 out of 5 of them were normally with their troops. As Jacob wrote: 'Every [British] officer of a native regiment of the line now endeavours to get away from his corps, to escape from regimental duty by every effort in his power. The *refuse* only is left.'

The other armies had much the same grievances as those in Bengal but almost without exception they remained loyal. In Madras one regiment was disbanded when it demurred at being ordered to embark for Bengal. In Bombay partial mutinies broke out in two battalions that were promptly disarmed, while a third, which showed signs of disaffection, was shipped off to garrison duty in Aden, where it behaved very well. The Punjab Irregular Force was loyal to a man and played a key role in defeating the rebels and in keeping the frontier peaceful.

In Bengal the picture was very different. Only a shadow of the former establishment remained. Apart from the Governor General's Bodyguard (which was at one time disarmed as a precaution) the Regular Cavalry had disappeared. The Irregular Cavalry was reduced from 18 regiments to 8. Sixty-two battalions of infantry mutinied or were disbanded on suspicion. Only 12 battalions of the line (21st, 31st, 32nd, 33rd, 42nd, 43rd, 47th, 59th, 63rd, 65th, 66th and 70th) and 6 'local' battalions (Kelat-i-Ghilzai Regiment, Shekhawati Battalion, Ferozepore Sikhs, Ludhiana Sikhs, Sirmoor Rifle Battalion (Gurkhas), Kumaon Battalion [Gurkhas]) remained.

The great Mutiny of 1857 at last convinced Britain that the government of a vast country could not be entrusted to a trading company that had not made a commercial transaction for more than 20 years. On 1 November 1858 a proclamation announced that the Queen had assumed the sovereignty of India. Automatically the Company's army became another royal army. Since the Company's troops had usually served under royal generals for the past century the immediate change was not very noticeable. The only ripple in the smooth transition concerned the Company's European regiments. It was decided that they should be transfered *en bloc* to the British Army. Many of the soldiers resented this. They claimed that they had enlisted for service in India only where, despite many climatic disadvantages, there were privileges not available to British troops in other parts of the world. They claimed that they should have the option of taking their discharge or of re-enlisting with the bounty payable to all recruits. Despite the advice of Commander-in-Chief, India, the government in Calcutta refused to concede this point. The viceroy was pressing a private policy of maintaining 30 European battalions specially recruited for India and was unwilling to release any Europeans to form a nucleus of this force. Serious trouble was narrowly averted. Some of the Europeans approached Sikh regiments to concert a plan to drive the royal army out of India. One European private was shot for mutiny and a compromise was reached. The 'white sepoys' were allowed to leave the service if they wished or to transfer to the royal army with two years' additional service to count towards pension instead of a bounty. Enough accepted transfer to enable 3 cavalry and 9 infantry units to be added to the British line.

Apart from the change in allegiance the main difference in the reformed army was that the number of British officers was cut from 24 to 6 in each Indian battalion. While it is true that one of the contributory causes of the Mutiny was the small number of officers present with the regular battalions, the irregular units had shown up very well and they had always had the lower establishment of British officers. The difference lay in the quality of the officers. The reduction in overall numbers would enable better candidates to be chosen. Moreover, it would do away with the idleness due to lack of occupation that had so sapped the enthusiasm of the Company's regimental officers. In future there would not only be more than enough for the remaining British officers to do, but more work would have to be devolved on to the Indian officers who, it was rightly believed, would thrive on increased responsibility. It was decided that in future the proportion of British regiments to Indian should not fall below one to three and that all artillery, except from some mountain batteries on the frontier, should be in British hands.

The old arrangement of having three separate Presidency armies was retained until the end of the century and the Punjab Irregular Force was maintained under civil control until 1886.

The reconstruction of the Bengal Army was a major operation. The cavalry was recreated by turning the 8 remaining irregular regiments into regular units with Skinner's Horse, founded in 1803, at the head of the line. Eleven additional regiments were added from units raised during the Mutiny. Most of these were Sikhs but a regiment from Rohilkund, one of Mahrattas from Gwalior and Murray's Jat Lancers were also included.

Much the same process was followed in reconstituting the infantry. The loyal regular regiments were renumbered 1 to 12 and they were followed by the 6 loyal local battalions. Then came 2 regiments, later known as the Regiment of Lucknow and the Loyal Regiment, composed of fractions of mutinied regiments who had refused to betray their officers. In the immediate reorganization promulgated in May 1861 the line was completed with 24 more battalions temporarily raised during the Mutiny. The great majority of these were designated as Punjab infantry, but a few were Sikhs and there were single battalions originally raised as levies in such places as Meerut, Delhi, Alighar and Gwalior. The shift of recruiting to the north-west was unmistakable.

Less than six months after the regiments had received their new numbers the policy was changed. It was decided to take the Gurkha regiments out of the line and number them separately. Thus the 11th (formerly 66th), 17th (Sirmoor), 18th (Kumaon) and 19th regiments of Bengal Native Infantry became the 1st to 4th Gurkhas and all the remaining Bengal battalions numbered 12 and above changed their numbers. This is one of the reasons why the histories of the various Indian regiments are so complicated, even apart from the major reforms of 1824, 1861, 1903 and 1922. The table of precedence of Indian regiments reads rather like a crossword puzzle. The other cause of confusion is the steady westward movement of the recruiting areas. As an example of the difficulties the 40th Bengal infantry may be quoted. It was raised in 1858 as the Shajahanpur levy in Rohilkund, 150 miles east of Delhi. In May 1861 it was mustered as the 44th of the Bengal line, but the removal of the Gurkha battalions in October of that year changed its number to 40. By 1890 its source of recruits had moved so far west that it was designated as 40th (Baluch), although Baluchistan was within the area of the Bombay Army. Two years later it became 40th (Pathan) Bengal Infantry, only to become 40th Punjab in 1901. In the reorganization of 1903 it reverted to 40th Pathans.

The confusion over the numbering and designation of regiments was nothing compared to the control organization that was fixed over the army after the Mutiny. The three commanders-in-chief in Bengal,

Madras and Bombay were retained, with the Bengal post having the title of Commander-in-Chief, India, although Madras and Bombay retained wide measures of independence that they seldom hesitated to use. To control all the generals there was a military branch of the civil government. The intention had been to erect in Calcutta an equivalent to the Secretary of State for War in London. This was to ensure civilian control over the army. By some singular ineptitude the head of the Military Department in India was always a soldier and junior to the Commander-in-Chief. He was in charge of all administration and, in particular, of supply and transport. He was a permanent member of the Viceroy's Council, while the C-in-C attended only by invitation. He was the Viceroy's chief military adviser. Since the Commander-in-Chief was always a full general and the Military Member was never more than a major general the system was fraught with trouble and friction, especially as the Member could be appointed without reference to the C-in-C.

To make matters worse, the Military Department wound itself into a bureaucratic cocoon. Sir John Adye quoted a case that he met in 1863:

An old officer called and requested me to give him a certificate of his being alive, as the audit department refused to give him his pension without it. He seemed to be well and lively and I therefore complied at once; and as his visit was in August, dated it accordingly. On looking at it, he remarked: 'Ah, you have dated it August. That is of no use. I have already sent them one of that kind, but what they require is a certificate that I was alive in July.'

It is astonishing that the dual-control system lasted as long as it did, particularly as the Military Department seems to have implemented it with a culpable lack of tact. Sir Horace Smith Dorrien, who was Adjutant General in Calcutta, recalled an occasion when the then commander-in-chief put forward a proposal for a minor reform in the establishments of cavalry regiments that would save money without reducing their fighting capacity. His only reply was a brief intimation, over the signature of a captain, that the government of India did not regard the change as desirable.

Two years later Lord Kitchener arrived as Commander-in-Chief. He took the existence of the Military Member as a personal affront. By nature an autocrat, Kitchener had just completed the dreary business of finishing off the Boer War. He was a great organizer, a mediocre administrator and the current military hero of the British public, a fact that had gone to his head. Lloyd George said he 'was like one of those revolving lighthouses which radiates momentary gleams of revealing light far into the surrounding gloom and then suddenly relapses into complete darkness'.

There was plenty of surrounding gloom in the organization of the Indian Army and Kitchener had been ordered to effect reforms. He took the Military Department as his first target and in consequence clashed irremediably with the Viceroy. Lord Curzon had welcomed his new Commander-in-Chief and was urgent that reforms should be made. Before Kitchener's arrival he had expressed a low opinion of the Military Department, saying that in it there flourished 'red tape, officialdom of the most rampant kind [and] an utterly vicious system of departmental finance'. Kitchener regarded the office-bound methods of the Department as so absurd that he set his aides-de-camp to pounding up their files into *papier-mâché* to make the mouldings for the ceiling of the palatial ceiling of the dining hall that he was adding, at the public expense, to his official residence at Simla. Curzon, however, rallied to the defence of the system he had derided and, before it was changed (for another quite as unsatisfactory), he was forced to resign.

Kitchener was more successful in some of his other reforms. At long last the presidency armies were abolished and with them the misleading territorial titles. There was little point in retaining a Madras title for a unit composed of Sikhs and Gurkhas formed for service in Burma. The infantry regiments of the whole force were numbered in a single series. The Bengal regiments took the head of the line (1 to 48), followed by the Punjab Frontier Force (51 to 59) and the Madras units (61 to 98). The Bombay regiments brought up the rear (101 to 130). The Gurkhas were listed separately and the infantry of the Guides were unnumbered. The cavalry were similarly treated. The Bengal regiments retained their numbers 1 to 19, the PFF took 21 to 25, Madras 26 to 28 and Bombay 31 to 37. The 2 regiments of Central India Horse, which had been rated as local horse (without a number), became 37 and 38 and the 3 regiments of Hyderabad Cavalry were fitted in as 20th, 29th and 30th. The Guides Cavalry continued unnumbered until the next re-organization in 1922. Simultaneously many out-of-date territorial titles were changed, 14 Madras regiments being renamed Punjabis.

He also tried to re-examine the purpose of the Indian Army. In its traditional deployment, scattered all over the subcontinent, it seemed to have two aims: to prevent a recurrence of the Mutiny, in itself an inadequate purpose for any military force; and to hold down the population. It was clear that the second aim was unnecessary and, if it became necessary, would be impossible. In the first decade of the twentieth century there was no likelihood of a large-scale rising against British rule. The princes had been brought into the system of government and were far from restive. The peasants were better off and more contented than they had been for centuries. The rising middle class, who had supported Britain whole-heartedly during the Mutiny, were not yet strong enough or disaffected enough to strive seriously for the independence they obtained in 1947. As late as 1914 Mahatma Gandhi could still assert: 'We can still enjoy freedom by continuing to live under the British flag.' If the civil population turned against their rulers on any massive scale there was little the army could do about it. There was only one soldier, Indian or British, to every 6,000 of the population and vast areas never saw a soldier from one year to the next.

Kitchener rejected the theory that the army's task was to occupy India. That he was right to do so is demonstrated by the fact that in 1914–18 the number of British troops needed to garrison India was only three-quarters of the number needed in 1811, when the war with Napoleon was at its height and British possessions were only a tithe of what they later became. Instead he decided to deploy and organize the army to meet an external menace. The terms of enlistment were altered so that future recruits would be liable to serve anywhere in India and the army was organized into permanent brigades and divisions. Since the menace Kitchener had in mind was a Russian invasion from the north-west, the bulk of the army was stationed in Sind and the Punjab. Working from an incorrect premise, he had set in train the reorganization which, with amendments, enabled the Indian Army to play such a distinguished part in the two world wars.

Kitchener was not alone in fearing an invasion from the north-west. Throughout the nineteenth century the appearance of a hostile European army on the Khyber Pass was a possibility that played a large part in British political and military thinking. In 1808 ambassadors were sent to the Sikh and Afghan courts seeking alliances against the possibility of a French corps crossing the Hindu Kush. To the classically educated British leaders of the day there was nothing improbable in the idea. Alexander of Macedon had reached the Indus; it was to be assumed that Napoleon Bonaparte could do the same. Napoleon's thinking had indeed been along these lines at the turn of the century and it may be that Sir Sidney Smith's defence of Acre prevented a French attempt to invade India in 1799. Such an attempt would certainly have failed, since neither Napoleon nor the British had appreciated the extent to which the fertility of Persia had decreased since Alexander's time.

When the French menace faded, the Russians took their place. Russia expanded rapidly to the east and south-east during the nineteenth century. The Czar and his ministers frequently made statements that could be, and were, read as threats to Afghanistan and India. In fact the Russian government would almost certainly have been deterred from engaging deliberately in war with Britain in India by the logistic problems involved. Their control over their generals in Turkestan was, however, far from complete and there was always a chance that an incident might occur without sanction from St Petersburg that might turn out to form a *casus belli*. In 1885 a Russian army defeated an Afghan force at Penjdeh, a fertile district that was probably outside the ill-defined Afghan frontier. The Russians annexed the area and laid claim to the Zufilkar Pass, which would give them easy access to Herat, an Afghan town they had long and openly coveted. Mr Gladstone, a prime minister not addicted to sabre-rattling, immediately asked and obtained from Parliament a credit of £11,000,000, in those days a sum sufficient to finance a fair-scale war. The threat was sufficient to check Russian ambitions for some time.

Whatever the actual potency of Russia's threat to India, its existence made relations with Afghanistan crucial to the government in Calcutta. It was a fixed principle that Kabul should be in the British sphere of influence and any hint of Russian intrigues there caused immediate alarm. There was never a British intention to annex the country, since it was realized that it would be a very prickly possession. What the British failed to realize was what a prickly possession it was to the Afghan rulers. They could never count on being in control of their own outlying tribes. They could seldom count on the loyalty of their own army and occasionally not even on the fidelity of their own commanders-in-chief. What the British took for perfidy was seldom more than the reluctance of successive amirs to admit that they were in no position to enforce adherence to obligations they had undertaken. As a result the British fought two very unsatisfactory wars with Afghanistan. The first ended with a disaster, the second began with one. Neither war achieved anything. In 1919 the Afghans invaded India but were repulsed without difficulty. Ten years later Russian troops – in Afghan uniforms – at last invaded Afghanistan, but when it was realized that the crisis in which they had come to meddle had been over for a fortnight they were quickly withdrawn.

Between Afghanistan and India lay the North-West Frontier, 700 miles of tangled mountainous country inhabited by 126 tribes and sub-tribes. When Britain inherited the problem of the frontier on the annexation of the Punjab, the area was in a state of chronic brigandage.

The Sikhs had endeavoured to collect revenue in the more accessible parts by what amounted to military expeditions. In return the hill men had made continuous raids into the plains. They could scratch little more than subsistence from their own country. Anything else, such as a dowry or a firearm (an essential adjunct in a society where the blood feud was endemic), had to come from those more fortunately situated. Since the tribes, though given to warring among themselves, were united in being Muslims, it was clearly desirable to do their looting among the infidel Sikhs or British than among their co-religionists.

The British soon learned that the problems of establishing peace and law in the frontier area were insuperable. They contented themselves with drawing an administrative border, further back than the international frontier. Behind this they ruled, collected taxes and administered the law. Beyond it they intervened only when they had no alternative. The number of interventions required is attested to by the fact that between 1849 and 1938 31 bars were issued to the various India General Service medals for operations on the North-West Frontier. One bar alone referred to 16 separate expeditions.

Fighting on the frontier had a special flavour of its own. It was conducted in deadly earnest and wounded men left in the tribesmen's hands were liable to suffer ghastly mutilations. At the same time there was something of a sporting contest about it. It is recorded that on one occasion a message was sent in to the British camp at the end of a day's fighting in which the tribesmen apologized for their poor shooting: they had discovered, too late, that their new rifles had been wrongly sighted. Political officers passed between the opposing forces with immunity. As early as 1863 an officer recalled that 'some of our native troops, when on isolated piquets at night, used to pass away the dreary hours by singing some of their native airs; and the enemy, apparently not wishing to be left out, would cheerily join in the chorus'.

Any campaign against an irregular army in broken country is a trying, exhausting and usually unsatisfactory business. On the frontier the enemy were skilful and brave, operating in country admirably suited to their tactics and at times at least as well armed as the regulars. What campaigning under these conditions could mean in terms of human exertion is illustrated by this description of the achievement of the Kashmir mountain gunners on the Chitral expedition of 1895:

Here were some two hundred and fifty men, Hindus and Mussulmans, who, working shoulder to shoulder, had brought two mountain guns, with their carriages and a supply of ammunition,* across some twenty miles of deep soft snow, across a pass some twelve thousand three hundred feet high, at the beginning of April, the worst time of the year. It must also be remembered that these men were also carrying their own rifles, great coats, and eighty rounds of ammunition, and wearing heavy sheepskin coats; they had slept for two days in the snow, and struggled from dawn to dark, sinking at every step up to their waists, and suffering acutely from a blinding glare and a bitter wind.

The political value of military operations on the frontier may have been questionable, but to the Indian Army it provided an invaluable training-ground, a field-firing range where both sides used live ammunition. In 1914 no army in the world had as much battle training as the Indian and the British units that served with it. Kitchener's reforms meant that in time every Indian unit did a turn of duty on the frontier. Sometimes the training aspect of the operations may have been a little overdone. An officer remembered seeing some newly raised tribal levies† in action in 1895:

The Levies opened fire at three hundred yards, rather close range to begin an action, and it was very amusing watching them; their instruction in volley firing had only just begun, but they had entire faith in its efficiency. The section commander used to give the word to load in their own language, but the order to fire was 'fira vollee' and they were supposed to fire on the word 'vollee'. If any man fired before the order – and they frequently did – the section commander used to rush at the culprit and slap him severely on the nearest part of him.

Commanding troops on the frontier demanded leadership and training of a very high standard, but commanding Indian troops even under peaceful conditions made some curious demands on British officers. One great character among the officers was Colonel Macdonald, who commanded the Deoli Irregular Force (later 42nd [Deoli] Infantry). He was immensely popular with his troops, partly because he raised in his unit what was probably the first Indian regimental pipe band and was always accompanied by his personal piper, a young Meena, 'who he called Fassifern; this youth was always in attendance on him

---

* The barrel and carriage of a gun each weighed 200 lb. The ammunition boxes weighed 125 lb each.

† Tribal levies under British officers were used to hold a cordon along the administrative frontier, the regulars being held back for large-scale operations.

and ready to strike up a tune when he called for it'. In 1871 he showed one of his officers:

> . . . a little artificial lake with a temple erected in the middle of it. He told me that the lake had been made and the temple had been built by the men to commemorate the grant of good conduct pay to them, and that when they had finished the question arose as to what object of worship they should install in it. They decided that it should be himself, but he absolutely refused his sanction to any such proposition, and before he knew of their intention they had substituted the regimental doctor for him. The doctor was on leave at the time, so that he had no opportunity of refusing the honour that was being conferred on him. An exceedingly good likeness of the doctor was fashioned in clay, was painted red (the orthodox colour for a god) and was duly placed in the temple with great ceremony before any of the British officers could interfere. 'Both I and the doctor,' added the colonel, 'considered the question of ordering the image's removal, but we came to the conclusion that to destroy one installed in a temple might create undesirable trouble. It moreover is a very good likeness, so we agreed it was best not to interfere. So there it is.'

The colonel of another battalion was less discreet. He discovered that for twenty-five years past an oral addition had been made to the standing orders of the native guard at Government House, Poona. This had been communicated regularly from one guard to another on relief and was to the effect that any cat passing out of the front door after dark was to be regarded as His Excellency the Governor and saluted accordingly:

> The meaning of this was that Sir Robert Grant, Governor of Bombay, had died there in 1838 and on the evening of the day of his death a cat was seen to leave the house by the front door and walk up and down a particular path as had been the Governor's habit to do after sunset. A Hindu sentry had observed this, and he mentioned it to others of his faith, who made it a subject of superstitious conjecture, the result being that one of the priestly class interpreted the circumstance to mean that the spirit of the deceased governor had entered into one of his household pets. It was difficult to fix on a particular one, and it was therefore decided that every cat passing out of the main entrance was to be regarded as the tabernacle of Governor Grant's soul and was to be treated with due respect and the proper honours. This decision was accepted without question

by all the native attendants and others belonging to Government House. The whole guard from sepoy to Subadar fully acquiesced in it, and an oral addition was made to the standing orders that the sentry at the front door would 'present arms' to any cat passing out there after dark. The notion was essentially Hindu, yet Mahomedans and native Christians and Jews devoutly assented to it. . . .

[The colonel] had the fullest belief in his ability to influence his men to dare the demons of darkness. . . . He set his mind firmly on this and he assembled the native officers and ordered them to refuse to take over, or countenance in any way, the unwritten order regarding the house cat, warning them of the severe court-martial consequences of disobedience. When the first guard furnished by his regiment after this warning returned from the week's duty at Government House, the Subadar in command was questioned regarding the oral order. It then came out that his fear of the supernatural was greater than his fear of the stern uncompromising colonel, and in his awful presence he meekly said . . . that to act as ordered meant to him a life of terror and a death of horror and, having disobeyed, he was ready to lose his highly prized commission and the pension reward for his long and faithful service.

Animals were liable to upset even the most stately occasion:
1st January 1877 saw the Queen proclaimed Empress of India. The ceremony was most imposing . . . tented pavillions had been constructed on an open plain. The throne pavillion in the centre was a very graceful erection, brilliant in hangings of red, blue and white satin, magnificently embroidered in gold . . . It was hexagonal in shape and rather more than two hundred feet in circumference. In front of this was the pavillion for the Ruling Chiefs and high European officials in the form of a semi circle, 800 feet long. . . .

The native Princes showed their loyalty not only by their homage but by taking part in the elephant procession, each Prince doing his best to show as much wealth as he possibly could. . . .

The arrival of the Viceroy was greeted by a salute of 101 guns with a *feu-de-joie* from the long line of troops. This was too much for the elephants . . . they became more and more alarmed and at last scampered off, dispersing the crowd in every direction.

Elephants were employed for moving the larger artillery pieces but could be troublesome if they had to be moved by sea, as happened when they were taken on the Abyssinian expedition of 1868. Sir Garnet Wolseley, in his invaluable *Soldier's Pocket Book* (1886 ed.), laid down that their rations on shipboard should be 'Atta [flour] or rice, 18 to 20 lbs, 170 lbs dry or 320 lbs green fodder, 2½ oz salt and 40 to 50 gallons of water. Three tons of sand for each elephant should be shipped for a thirty day voyage. Elephants should be placed tail to tail, with their heads to the ship's side.'

To the Indian soldier the most remarkable thing about his British officer was his wife. Subadar Sitaram remarked in his memoirs that his religious teacher had told him: 'Put not your trust in the counsels of women for they are like ice; firm in the morning but melting as the sun shines.' But, said Sitaram, 'he had never seen an English memsahib'.

To judge from an equivalent to Mrs Beeton prepared in 1898 for ladies going to India, the potential memsahib must have found India almost as imposing as the Indians found her:

The first duty of the mistress is, of course, to be able to give intelligible orders to her servants; it is therefore necessary she should learn to speak Hindustani. . . .

She is primarily responsible for the decency and health of all persons living in her service. With this object she should insist upon her servants living in their quarters, and not in the bazaar; but this, on the other hand, is no reason why they should turn your domain into a caravanserai for their relations to the third and fourth generation . . . it is well to draw a very sharp line in this respect. . . .

The ordinary Indian cook has not an idea for breakfast beyond chops, steaks, fried fish and quail . . . there should be at least two plates of butter and toast. With regard to the former, the *khitmugar* should generally be discouraged from making it the medium for a display of his powers in the plastic art; it is doubtless gratifying to observe such yearning after beauty, even in butter, but it is suggestive of too much handling to be pleasant, . . .

Luncheon . . . is not a set meal and the courses need not be observed strictly . . . It is absurd to see people sitting at lunch or breakfast with empty plates, because someone is eating an entrée. Heavy luncheons or tiffins have much to answer for in India. . . .

The first axiom for camp is not to do without comfort. The mistress will find it convenient to have a pair of light camel trunks for clothes. . . . a few cane chairs with wadded covers, little tables and table cloths, and a shelf or two will give a home look to the sitting tent . . . The silver should be carried in baize or flannel hold-alls . . . if you keep cows it is better to let them go into camp with you, so there should be no difficulty in making butter.

The annual retreat to the cool of the hills required the memsahib to be a genius at organization. The movement of a family 'consisting of a lady, three children and an English nurse', was calculated to require eleven camels, exclusive of breakables, which 'are preferably carried on mules'. The recommended load for the seventh camel comprised: 'Two boxes containing house linen, two casks containing ornaments, purdah bamboos, tennis poles.' The eleventh camel should carry 'drawing room sundries, servants' coats, iron bath, cheval glass, plate basket'. Sir Garnet advised that a camel should be loaded with 'from 300 to 480 lbs (not counting the saddle)'. He added that while an unladen camel occupied 25 square feet, a loaded beast needed 70 square feet.

The author of this compendium did not expect the memsahib to be quite omnicompetent: 'When the time comes for loading up, retire gracefully.'

If every family required eleven camels (apart from those families who took their pianos, which 'must be carried by coolies, of whom 14 or 16 will be required'), the move of the viceroy and the commander-in-chief to Simla was a stupendous operation. As Lord Roberts recalled,

> . . . the followers, as a rule, are accompanied by their wives and families . . . there could not have been less than 20,000 men, women and children, a motley crowd streaming along four-and-twenty miles of road, for the day's march was usually about twelve miles, and before everyone had cleared out of the camp occupied the night before, the advance guard had begun to arrive on the ground to be occupied the next day.

Simla was depicted by Rudyard Kipling as the home of tittle-tattle and amorous intrigue. Far more complications were caused by questions of social protocol. One officer, writing of 1874, remarked:

> The tranquillity of social life is often disturbed by polemics arising out of questions of precedence. In India it depends almost entirely upon military rank, and so as to regulate it as between officers of the army and civil servants, all gazetted officers doing duty in the civil service are given relative military rank. But the standing of individuals is often ambiguous and this frequently leads to unseemly quarrels among them. I was present at a small private dinner party at which our host took in a lady who ranked as a major, unaware that among his guests there was another lady who ranked as a lieutenant colonel. The female lieutenant colonel was furious at her junior preceding her, and she showed it by refusing to speak, to eat or to drink during the meal; then when the wine

went round, she abruptly left the table, strode to the door, called for her carriage and departed without saying good night to anybody. Early next morning our host received an official letter from the lady's husband informing him that he would be reported to superior authority for grossly insulting his (the lady's husband's) wife.

If one was sufficiently senior such questions were unlikely to occur and Lord Lytton, Viceroy in the seventies, took a different, if no less jaundiced, view of life in Simla: 'Members of the Council and heads of departments hold prayer meetings at each others' houses three times a week and pass the remainder of their time in writing spiteful minutes against each other.' From this it would appear that the wife of one of his predecessors, Lady William Bentinck, had not succeeded in her purpose when she converted the Simla billiard hall into a church. Had she not done so it is possible that snooker would have been invented there. As it was the rules of the game were devised in the Ootacamund Club in Madras by Captain Neville Chamberlain.

Whatever their rank and good intentions neither Lady William nor any of the vicereines can rank as the most memorable of the memsahibs. That title must be awarded to a lady who did not spend much of her married life in India. She was Marie Dolores Eliza Rosanna Gilbert, daughter of an ensign in the British 44th Regiment. At Simla in 1837, when she was nineteen, she married Lieutenant James of the 22nd Bengal Native Infantry. She made at least three more marriages and at one time had to move to Spain to avoid prosecution for bigamy, a danger averted when one of her husbands was accidentally drowned. Her greatest triumphs were, however, extramarital. She became a star dancer in London, Berlin, Dresden, Paris, St Petersburg and Warsaw, but she made her greatest impression in Munich. The King of Bavaria was so obsessed with her that she controlled his government for two years. She became Gräfin von Lansfelt in the peerage of Bavaria, but the world remembers her as Lola Montez.

7th Bengal Cavalry, 1890.

The plates have been arranged in four sections, representing the four major periods of the Indian Army, though the sections are of uneven length and do not reflect either the size of the army at the time or the length of time that the period lasted. The first short section depicts the Company's army between the Napoleonic Wars and the Indian Mutiny. In this section the uniforms are very closely modelled on British practice. The second and longest section covers the four armies between the Mutiny and the Kitchener reorganization of 1902–3. That is followed by the unified army that emerged from that reform and lasted until 1922, when a further gigantic reorganization took place. The fourth section of only three plates shows the full-dress uniforms which, for very ceremonial purposes only, lasted until Independence. Within the sections the plates are arranged chronologically, except that in sections 2 and 3 the cavalry precede the infantry. An essay on 'Uniforms and Soldiers' falls between plates 27–28.

The Plates

The Company's Army

PLATE 1
21st Bengal Native Infantry
(1819)

This picture of a subadar shows how closely the Indian Army followed the British, even if they were usually a reform or two behind current British practice. His jacket is of a design abandoned by the British about fifteen years earlier. The shako, however, approximates to the British pattern of late 1815 (the 'Prussian' shako), although it is worn without a peak.

This officer belongs to the light or skirmishing company, as is shown by his elaborate 'wings' as opposed to the counter-epaulettes of the battalion companies. He carries the curved light infantry officer's sword and the green light infantry ball tuft in his shako.

The main differences from British usage are that the sword is suspended from a frog attached to the shoulder-belt whereas a British light company officer would have worn it suspended from slings. The subadar is wearing a kummerbund rather than the net sash of the same colour that a British officer would have worn.

The dress of the other ranks of the Native Infantry would also have resembled their British equivalents down to the waist. Below that they wore abbreviated shorts, about the same length as those now favoured by male tennis-players, with a black dog's-tooth pattern round the lower edge. Their legs were bare but they wore light shoes without laces. Havildars (sergeants) wore breeches like those of the officers.

The 21st Native Infantry were the senior regiment of the Bengal line to remain loyal during the Mutiny. In 1861 they were renumbered as the 1st Native Infantry, becoming the 1st Brahman Infantry in 1901. The facings remained yellow until 1886, when they became white. The lace changed from silver to gold in 1831.

Chater captioned this picture 'Calcutta Native Militia, 1795'. In this he followed a drawing of A. C. Lovett. The original source material is almost certainly a print of the 21st BNI by Captain Williams, executed in 1819.

PLATE 2
Madras Light Cavalry
(1847)

British officers in the Indian Army almost always had a special uniform prescribed for them in *Dress Regulations* but increasingly tended to wear the dress laid down for the Indian officers, with or without minor modifications.

This British officer of Madras Light Cavalry is dressed according to the book. His French-grey jacket and sky-blue trousers combine articles from both hussar and light dragoon dress in the British service. The jacket with its elaborate silver lacing across the chest comes from the hussars. So does the 'barrelled' sash. The headdress, on the other hand, was taken from the light dragoons, although the hussars had also worn it between 1822 and 1842. This was the shako adopted in 1812 despite Wellington's protests that it made it impossible to tell the difference between French and British light cavalry. The Madras cavalry, however, did not adopt it until 1846. They had previously worn a heavy dragoon helmet similar to that in plate 3.

The cap badge, which is partly obscured by the cap scales, is a Maltese cross, surmounted by a crown and with the letters MLC (Madras Light Cavalry) in the centre. Distinctions between the eight regiments of MLC were hard to find. All wore pale buff facings. It seems that to tell one from the other it was necessary to look closely at the officers' sabretaches. On these were worn the regimental number and authorized battle honours. The 4th, 5th and 7th regiments had the honour *Assaye* and an elephant to commemorate Arthur Wellesley's victory over the Mahrattas in 1803.

PLATE 3
Bombay Horse Artillery
(1848)

Although this British officer wears the blue jacket faced with red that was the hallmark of almost all European artillerymen, he could more easily be taken for a dragoon of the Second Empire than an officer of Bombay Horse Artillery. This impression is heightened by the red stripe on the white trousers which is not authorised in the Regulations.

Since the front of the jacket does not show in the picture it is worth quoting the *Regulations* on the subject. These call for a

> ... blue cloth round shell [jacket], scarlet Prussian collar three inches deep; laced entirely round the edge with one inch wide gold lace, ornamented with a border of narrow Russia braid and on the collar with a border of small Russia figuring; single breasted with five rows of Ordnance buttons, centre row balls, the others half balls, richly trimmed with thick gold square braid loops extending the full width of the jacket across the breast and about three inches wide at the bottom; pointed cuffs three inches deep, ornamented in the same way as the collar with gold Russia braid and rounded off to form of cuff; the back is also ornamented up the seams with one inch wide gold lace with an edging of narrow Russia braid; crimson silk lining.

Even with white linen trousers, it must have been a very uncomfortable uniform to wear in Bombay.

The jacket closely resembled that used by British Horse Gunners but the helmet was, for artillerymen, purely an Indian adornment. With its elegant classical shape and gilt ornamentation it was taken into use by most European heavy cavalry during the Napoleonic Wars, with either the floating horsehair crest or with what the French call a *chenille* or caterpillar. A similar helmet was also worn, with more regard for history than comfort, by the officers of the Duke of York's Greek Light Infantry.

This is the only plate of artillery in the book, since at the Mutiny all Indian artillery, except some mountain batteries on the frontier, was abolished and not revived until 1936.

1858–1902
(CAVALRY)
PLATE 4
13th Bengal Lancers
(1882)

Two officers of the 13th Bengal Lancers came to England in 1882 for the victory celebrations after the battle of Tel-el-Kebir against the Egyptians. A picture of them appeared in the *Illustrated London News* and one of them, Risaldar Hussein Ali Khan, is depicted in precisely the same uniform as is shown in this plate, except for a detail in the top of the boots. There is another portrait of Ali Khan in the Queen's Collection. This shows him wearing blue breeches and was painted by General Fane of Fane's Horse (19th Bengal Lancers).

The 13th Lancers were raised at Lahore in 1858 as the 4th Sikh Irregular Cavalry. Their first second-in-command was Lieutenant John Watson VC. They became 13th Bengal Cavalry in 1861 and were converted to Lancers three years later. In 1884 they received the additional title 'Duke of Connaught's', the Duke having also taken part in the Egyptian campaign in command of a brigade of infantry. The presidency title was dropped in 1903, so they became 13th Duke of Connaught's Lancers; the suffix 'Watson's Horse' was added three years later. It is suitable that the name of Colonel John Watson should be commemorated since, apart from his other exploits, he made a little-known contribution to the comfort of cavalrymen: it was he who introduced the practice of rising in the stirrups while trotting on all but ceremonial occasions. Previously military horsemen had bumped the saddle on all occasions.

Despite all their changes of title the regiment retained a blue uniform with red facings, silver lace and a Kashmir-style kummerbund.

The two decorations worn are the Egyptian medal (1882–9) and the Khedival star for the same campaign. In Fane's portrait Ali Khan is shown wearing the medals for the Indian Mutiny and the Second Afghan War.

PLATE 5
1st Bombay Lancers
(1887)

Raised in 1817, the senior cavalry unit of the Bombay army, they were originally a regiment of Light Cavalry but took the suffix '(Lancers)' in 1842. This was dropped twenty years later, only to reappear in 1880, when the unit were entitled 1st Bombay Lancers. Ten years later, when the Duke ended his two-year term as Commander-in-Chief, Bombay, they became the Duke of Connaught's Own. Like all the Bombay cavalry regiments 30 was added to their number in 1903 and they then became 31st Duke of Connaught's Own Lancers. In the 1922 reorganization they were amalgamated with the 2nd (later 32nd) Bombay Lancers to form the 13th Duke of Connaught's Own Lancers. This is confusing in view of the subject of plate 4, the 13th Duke of Connaught's Bengal Lancers, who in 1922 amalgamated with the 16th Cavalry to form the 6th Duke of Connaught's Own Lancers.

If the 1st Bombay Lancers kept their number for more than eighty years they made up for it by a bewildering series of changes in uniform. When first raised they wore scarlet with white facings and gold lace but within three years they had changed to orange facings and silver lace. Silver lace survived the next change in 1826, when the uniform became French-grey and the facings reverted to white. These colours were retained for some time but the style changed from light dragoon to lancer in 1846 and back again in 1861. The facings became dark-blue in 1878. Everything changed in 1883. The European-style jacket was abandoned and a kurta adopted in its place. This was dark green with red facings and gold lace and lasted until 1903, when the kurta became blue with scarlet facings.

One characteristic of Bombay cavalry was that they had whistles on the chains of their shoulder-belts instead of the more usual 'pickers'.

Although the artist dated this picture 1887 and the uniform is correct for this date, the pose and details suggest that his source was a photograph dated ten years later.*

* Reproduced in A. H. Bowling, *Indian Cavalry Regiments 1880–1914* (London 1971), p. 58.

PLATE 6
1st Madras Lancers
(1887)

The regiment was formed in 1787 as 5th Native Cavalry and became 1st Madras Light Cavalry in the following year. They were converted to Lancers in 1886. In the consolidation of 1903 all Madras cavalry units added 25 to their numbers, so the regiment then became the 26th. At the same time they reverted to being a light cavalry regiment rather than Lancers. They received the distinction 'Prince of Wales's Own' in 1906 when the heir to the throne visited India. This title was changed to 'King George's Own' when the Prince came to the throne in 1910. In 1922 they were amalgamated with the 30th Lancers (Gordon's Horse), one of the former Hyderabad regiments, to form 8th King George's Own Light Cavalry.

Like other Madras regiments (see plate 2) the 1st Lancers wore French-grey with buff facings and silver lace. The Madras regiments also favoured the alkalak, a long tunic fastening on the chest, a shorter garment than the kurta worn in the rest of India. The curved lace on the chest is a characteristic of the alkalak.

According to the *Dress Regulations* the kummerbund should be of the same colours as the pugri. This picture, however, is unquestionably based on a havildar who visited Britain for the opening of the Imperial Institute in 1893. This NCO is shown in much the same pose as here in a photograph published in the *Navy and Army Illustrated* of 5 June 1896. The havildar is also wearing a red and gold kummerbund and a pugri similar to the one in this plate. This is also shown in a contemporary group of Indian NCOs taken at Buckingham Palace. In this group, as in Chater's picture, the sword is being carried detached from the frog, although it seems to be secured in the picture in the *Navy and Army Illustrated*.

In all three representations the subject wears the Indian General Service Medal 1854–95 with two bars. One of these bars would be for Burma 1885–7.

PLATE 7
5th Bombay Cavalry (Scinde Horse) (1888)

In 1839 a cavalry unit known as the Scinde Irregular Horse was raised by Lieutenant Clarke. It was not formed in Sind itself but was intended to police the border of that territory in the Rann of Kutch, a singularly inhospitable desert south of Karachi. Since the temperature here frequently reaches 135°F, it is astonishing to learn that in the early days the British officers wore tall white metal helmets, not unlike those worn today by the Household Cavalry, with a black plume.

When Clarke was killed in action the command passed to John Jacob and it was in his day that the unit was divided into two regiments, both having the suffix 'Jacob-ka-Risallah', which was retained until 1888. The 1st Regiment was taken into the Bombay line as the 5th Regiment in 1885, adding the name Scinde Horse three years later. In 1903 it was retitled 35th Scinde Horse and was reunited with its junior regiment in 1922 as the Scinde Horse (14th Prince of Wales's Own Cavalry).

The uniform was green with silver lace from 1857. The lace was changed to gold in 1898. The facings were white, except between 1882 and 1888 when they were scarlet. Throughout, however, the cloth under the shoulder-chains was scarlet.

PLATE 8
6th Bombay Cavalry (Jacob's Horse)
(1888)

This was the 2nd Regiment of the Scinde Horse (referred to in plate 7) and became 6th Bombay Cavalry (*Jacob-ka-Risallah*) in 1885. It shared with 5th Scinde Horse the early battle honours of *Cutchee*, *Meanee* and *Hyderabad*. It became 36th Jacob's Horse in 1903.

The uniform was green with silver lace, the latter becoming gold in 1870. The facings were primrose, except between 1882 and 1888 when, like the underside of the shoulder-chains, they were scarlet.

The model for this plate was a photograph of Risaldar Major Faiz Khan, who wears the medal for the Second Afghan War, 1878–80.

PLATE 9

11th (Prince of Wales's Own) Bengal Lancers (1890)

Soon after the Guides arrived to reinforce the British and loyal Indian troops grimly hanging on to the Delhi ridge in 1857, they were followed by two regiments of Sikh Irregular Cavalry dispatched from the Punjab by Sir John Lawrence. The senior of these two regiments were known as Wale's Horse until their commander was killed in the following year. His successor was Captain Dighton Probyn, who had won the VC at Agra. Thenceforward the regiment were known, through a good deal of name-changing, as Probyn's Horse, although the name was not made official until 1904, when it became the 11th Prince of Wales's Own Lancers (Probyn's Horse). Their old commander, by that time Major General the Rt Hon. Sir Dighton Probyn VC, PC, became colonel of the regiment in 1904 and held that position until his death at the age of ninety-two in 1924. Two years earlier the regiment had been amalgamated with the 12th Cavalry (formerly 2nd Sikh Irregular Horse) to form Probyn's Horse, 5th King Edward's Own Lancers.

From 1870 onwards Probyn's Horse had the same colours for their uniform – blue with red facings and gold lace.

Chater dated this picture 1890 but it is probable that the actual date of the uniforms is rather later. Lieutenant Colonel (later Field Marshal Lord) Birdwood, who commanded the regiment at the turn of the century, wrote in a note preserved at Sandhurst that the 11th Lancers were one of the last regiments to adopt khaki and went on active service as late as 1895 wearing blue kurtas. Another indication that the date is later than suggested is that the naik in blue would have been wearing a silver badge of the Prince of Wales's feathers up to 1905, when the regiment's title changed to King Edward's Own.

PLATE 10
2nd Madras Lancers
(1890)

The numbering of the Madras cavalry was early bedevilled by a quixotic ruling by the Council of Madras that their regiments should take their precedence not from the date of their raising but from the seniority of their commanding officer at the time. Thus this regiment were formed in 1784 as 3rd Native Cavalry, became 1st in the same year and slipped back to 4th in 1786. It was not until 1788 that they became the 2nd, a number they retained until 1902 when, adding 25 like the rest of the Madras cavalry, they became the 27th Light Cavalry. They were not amalgamated in 1922 but were renumbered as 16th Light Cavalry. From 1817 to 1922 their uniform was French grey with buff facing and silver lace (see plate 39).

The kot-daffadar in the plate wears a grey serge alkalak that opens all down the front. Over it is the Mackenzie leather equipment. The breeches are sky-blue with two white cloth stripes down the sides.

The source material for the plate must have been a photograph in the *Navy and Army Illustrated* for 28 January 1899, which it follows closely though with one curious deviation. According to the *Dress Regulations* the pugri should be blue, French-grey and white with gold according to rank. The 1899 photograph, although in black and white, seems to follow this rule, but for some reason Chater has shown a pugri that is predominantly red. The member of the same regiment shown in plate 16 wears a regulation pugri.

PLATE 11
3rd (Queen's Own) Bombay Light Cavalry (1890)

This regiment was taken into the Company's service as the 3rd Bombay Light Cavalry in 1820 but had previously been a unit raised by the Peshwa of Poona in 1817 and commanded by HEIC officers. In 1820 they consisted of ten risallahs (squadrons) each of five hundred men. One of these risallahs was composed of men from Skinner's Horse (see plate 29).

The 3rd Bombay Light Cavalry (then called Silladar Light Cavalry) took part in the Persian campaign of 1856–7 and at Kush-ab charged through three Persian infantry battalions. This won two officers the VC, the only time the cross had been awarded for an action on Persian soil. They captured a Persian standard surmounted by a silver hand, which was later worn on top of the staff of the regimental standard. NCOs also wore a small silver hand above their chevrons.

The Queen's Own had more uniform changes than usual, as the following list shows:

	Uniform	Facings	Lace
1823	scarlet	orange	silver
1826	French-grey	white	silver
1876	French-grey	scarlet	silver
1883	dark-green	scarlet	gold
1903	blue	scarlet	gold

The title 'Queen's Own' was added in 1876 and in 1903 the regiment became 33rd Queen's Own Light Cavalry. In 1922 they were amalgamated with the 4th (Prince Albert Victor's Own) Bombay Cavalry (Poona Horse) to form the Poona Horse (17th Queen Victoria's Own Cavalry).

PLATE 12
Central India Horse
(1893)

The most difficult part of the suppression of the Mutiny was the pacification of Central India, an anti-guerrilla operation on the largest scale. To assist in this campaign three regiments were raised, of which the first consisted of loyal cavalrymen from two mutinied Gwalior regiments together with Sikhs from the partly mutinied contingents from Malwa, Bhopal and Kotah. This unit was known as Mayne's Horse. After the pacification the three regiments together with men of the Mynpoorie Levy, another emergency unit, were formed into the two regiments of Central India Horse. They were intended to police the countryside they had pacified and were initially responsible to the civil authorities at Indore rather than to the commander-in-chief. However, the recruits were enlisted for service all over India and in 1879 they took part in the Afghan War. After 1860 the uniform of both regiments was drab, with maroon facings and gold lace. They became the 38th and 39th King George's Own Central India Horse in 1903 and were amalgamated into the Central India Horse (21st King George's Own Horse) in 1922.

Although they were never officially designated as 'Somebody's Horse', after 1860 their commanding officers included Henry Daly, Sam Browne vc, Dighton Probyn vc and John Watson vc, all of whom had regiments named after them.

The daffadar in the plate was the representative of the regiment who visited London for the opening of the Imperial Institute in 1893. There is a photograph of him in this pose in the *Navy and Army Illustrated* for 3 April 1896.

st Duke of York's Own Lancers (SKINNER'S HORSE)

nd Cavalry (GARDNER'S HORSE)

rd SKINNER'S HORSE

th Cavalry

th Cavalry

th Cavalry

th ~~Cavalry~~ Hariana Lancers

th Cavalry

th Bengal Lancers (HODSON'S HORSE)

th Bengal Lancers (HODSON'S HORSE)

th Prince of Wales's Own Lancers (PROBYN'S HORSE)

th Cavalry

th Duke of Connaught's Lancers (WATSON'S HORSE)

4th

5th

5th Cavalry

7th Cavalry

8th Tiwana Lancers → P of W's Own Lh → K.G.'s Own Lh.

9th Bengal Lancers (FANE'S HORSE)

th

1st Prince Albert's Own Cavalry (Frontier Force) (DALY'S HORSE)

2nd Punjab Cavalry

3rd Punjab Cavalry

4th

5th Cavalry (Frontier Force)

6th King George's Own Light Cavalry

7th Light Cavalry

8th

9th

th Lancers (GORDON'S HORSE)

1st Duke of Connaught's Own Lancers

2nd Bombay Lancers

3rd Queen's Own Light Cavalry

4th Prince Albert Victor's Own Cavalry (POONA HORSE)

5th SCINDE HORSE

6th JACOB'S HORSE

7th Lancers (BALUCH HORSE)

8th King George's Own Central India Horse

9th King George's Own Central India Horse

DOTTY BROWN

PLATE 13
5th Cavalry, Punjab Frontier Force
(1897)

The junior of the five original Punjab cavalry regiments was raised at Multan in 1849 by Captain Robert Fitzgerald of the 12th Bombay Native Infantry. They took part in the suppression of the Mutiny and were awarded the battle honours *Delhi* and *Lucknow*. They were renumbered 25th Cavalry (Frontier Force) in 1903 and amalgamated in 1922 with the 2nd (later 22nd) Punjab Cavalry to form Sam Browne's Cavalry, 12th Frontier Force.

Until 1922 their uniform was always green but the shade became steadily darker. It was officially described as dark-green by 1870 and although this description remained valid the cloth was indistinguishable from black by 1913.

This plate is based on photographs of Risaldar Major Kesur Singh, who visited England in 1897 for Queen Victoria's diamond jubilee. In honour of the occasion he wore a kummerbund with a red and gold striped end rather than the Kashmir pattern that was prescribed. He also wore white breeches rather than loose trousers of grey fustian.

It was a characteristic of the regiment that the officers carried mameluke hilted swords that were otherwise carried only by regimental officers in 4th Bengal Cavalry and Probyn's Horse.

PLATE 14
7th Bengal Cavalry
(1897)

In 1846 eight regiments of Irregular Cavalry (numbered 11–17) were raised in the Bengal Presidency for the Sikh war. In the following year their numbering was changed as the Bundelkund Legion, raised in 1838, was mustered as the 10th Irregular cavalry. Only the two junior of these regiments survived the Mutiny becoming regular cavalry as the 7th and 8th Bengal Cavalry. The 7th were converted to lancers in 1900 and since many of their recruits came from the district between the Jumna and Sutlej rivers they were officially entitled the 7th Hariana Lancers in 1904. They were amalgamated with 6th Bengal Cavalry in 1922 to form 18th King Edward's Own Cavalry.

From 1861 to 1922 they wore scarlet uniforms with blue facings and gold lace. The officer represented in the plate is Risaldar Neb Ram who attended the diamond jubilee. The special distinctions of the uniform are the broad lace down the front of the kurta, the gold piping on the flaps of the pockets and the shoulder strap. The 4th and 5th Bengal Cavalry had the whole of the breast pocket piped in gold (see Plate 17) but the 7th was unique in having only the flap piped. The shoulder strap was worn over the right shoulder and buckles to the waist belt on the left hip where it helps to support the weight of the sword (which is suspended from the belt by slings). It is in fact a Sam Browne belt covered in gold lace but ending in slings rather than a frog. The regiment abandoned this unusual item soon after the jubilee and their representative at the coronation of 1911 wore the more conventional shoulder belt.

PLATE 15
8th Bengal Cavalry
(1897)

The 8th Bengal Cavalry's origins were referred to in the note on plate 14. Like the 7th Cavalry, the 8th were converted to lancers in 1900 but changed back to cavalry four years later. In 1922 they joined 5th (Bengal) Cavalry to form 3rd Cavalry.

The regiment's representative at the Diamond Jubilee was Risaldar Makdul Khan. Unusually he wore short white gloves instead of the more usual gauntlets and two (unpiped) breast pockets. Chater almost certainly used a picture of him as a basis for this plate but, for some unexplained reason, gave him blue facings instead of red which the risaldar correctly wore.

PLATE 16
2nd Madras Lancers
(1900)

The background information about this regiment has been given under plate 10. The daffadar in this plate, however, is wearing the pugri laid down in the regulations and is in correct full dress for other ranks at the turn of the century.

PLATE 17
5th Bengal Cavalry
(1901)

Raised at Bareilly in 1841 as the 7th Bengal Irregular Cavalry, the regiment took part in the Sikh Wars and were present at the siege of Multan. After the Mutiny they became a regular regiment as 5th Bengal Cavalry, a number they retained until 1922, when they were amalgamated with the 8th Regiment (see plate 15) to form the 3rd Cavalry.

The 5th had a red uniform with gold lace from 1861 and blue facings were added in 1870. They were also distinguished by scroll-like elaborations of lace round the collar and down the chest opening.

However, the subject of this plate is a British officer, who, in this regiment, did not wear the facings. He is moreover in undress and thus does not wear the full quota of gold lace.

PLATE 18

9th Bengal Lancers (Hodson's Horse) (1902)

William Stephen Raikes Hodson was unusual for a Company officer since he had a degree from Trinity College, Cambridge at a time when higher education was uncommon in the Company's forces, or indeed in the royal army. In 1857 he commanded a large unit comprised of rissalahs raised by Sikh magnates round Amritsar and Lahore. This unit served prominently at the taking of Delhi and were then divided into two regiments, known as 1st and 2nd Hodson's Horse, which took part in the reliefs of both Cawnpore and Lucknow, at the last of which Hodson was killed.

In 1861 the two regiments were rated as 9th and 10th Bengal Cavalry. The suffix 'Hodson's Horse' was added to both in 1901. In 1922 the two were reunited as Hodson's Horse, 4th Duke of Cambridge's Own Lancers.

Both regiments wore salmon-coloured clothing from 1861 until they changed to blue with red facings in 1874. The 9th adopted white facings in 1887.

Risaldar Nadir Khan came to London for the Jubilee of 1897 and there was a photograph of him in the *Navy and Army Illustrated* for 27 December 1897. There is also a waist-length portrait of him by Rudolf Swoboda among Her Majesty's pictures. Chater probably used the photograph for details of uniform but took the face from elsewhere, since Nadir Khan was clean-shaven except for a Chinese-style moustache. He also wears four medals whereas the subject of the plate has only the medal for Egypt 1882–9 and the Khedival Star, since the 9th Bengal Lancers served at Suakim in 1885.

(INFANTRY)

PLATE 19
The Queen's Own Corps of Guides, Infantry, Punjab Frontier Force
(1887)

The raising of the Guides by Harry Lumsden has already been referred to (see p. 11), as has the introduction by the Guides of the use of khaki (see p. 101).

Lumsden's ideas for an inconspicuous uniform were retained almost in their entirety. In the cavalry of the Guides the officers took to wearing inconspicuous braiding across their chests in full dress. They also adopted facings of red velvet and blue and gold pugris. The whole effect, however, was markedly drab. The infantry stuck even more closely to Lumsden's scheme. They added red piping to their tunics and wound their khaki pugris round scarlet kullahs. For many years they even eschewed the scarlet kummerbund that the cavalry had worn from the beginning.

The Guides remained a distinct unit of both arms, neither cavalry nor infantry being numbered, until 1922. Then the cavalry became 10th Queen Victoria's Own Corps of Guides Cavalry (Frontier Force) and the infantry became 5th Battalion, 12th Frontier Force Regiment (Queen Victoria's Own Corps of Guides).

PLATE 20
1st Infantry, Punjab Frontier Force (1889)

In 1849, when the two Sikh Wars had ended in the annexation of the Punjab, 6 regiments of infantry and 5 regiments of cavalry were raised as the Transfrontier Brigade, later called the Punjab Irregular Force (known as the Piffers).

The first 5 of the infantry units were recruited from disbanded Sikh troops and the 6th by the conversion of the Scinde Camel Corps.

The 3rd Infantry, PIF was disbanded in 1882 but its number was left blank in the list. Although no space was left for it when the battalions were renumbered as 55th to 59th Rifles in 1902, the number was again left blank when they were regrouped as the 1st, 2nd, 4th, 5th and 6th battalions of the 13th Frontier Force Rifles in 1922.

While all the other battalions took to wearing khaki with facings of black, green, Prussian-blue, emerald-green and red, the 1st Battalion, which was described officially as Coke's Rifles from 1903, adopted the uniform of British riflemen. Their uniform was rifle-green with black lace and the red facings of the 60th (King's Royal Rifle Corps). They even adopted the shoulder-belt with the Maltese cross and the black buttons with embossed bugle horns.

Like the 42nd (Deoli) infantry (see page 28), Coke's Rifles claimed to have had the first regimental pipe band in the Indian Army.

PLATE 21
26th (Baluchistan) Bombay Infantry (1892)

The 26th Baluchs are an example of the north-western drift of recruitment for the Indian Army as the nineteenth century progressed. They were raised as an extra battalion in 1825 and taken into the Bombay line as the 26th Bombay Native Infantry in the following year. Their source of recruits was the west coast of central India. At that time the uniform was red with light buff facings and gold lace. Napier's conquest of Sind in the forties opened up access to Baluchistan on the borders of India and Persia. A special Baluch battalion (later the 27th Bombay Infantry) were raised in 1844 and increasingly Baluchistan became one of the greater sources of recruits for the Bombay army.

In 1892 this trend was acknowledged in the 26th and they were reclassified as the 26th (Baluchistan) Infantry. At the same time the uniform was changed to drab with red facings, the latter echoing the distinctive red trousers, a Baluchi feature, that were introduced at the same time.

The regiment became 126th Baluchistan Infantry in 1903 and 2nd Battalion 10th Baluchistan Regiment in 1922, the 1st Battalion of that regiment being the former 24th Bombay Infantry, which had been recognized as a Baluchi unit in 1891.

PLATE 22
15th Bengal Native Infantry (Ludhiana Sikhs) (1893)

After the First Sikh War the Jullundur Doab, the triangle of land between the Sutlej and Beas rivers, was ceded to the East India Company. Two Sikh regiments were raised there in 1846 from disbanded Sikh troops. The two units were assembled at the towns of Ferozepore and Ludhiana. Although both were originally intended for local service, they were dressed in the red jackets of regular troops, the Ferozepore regiment having yellow facings (see plate 37), the Ludhiana green.

Both regiments remained loyal during the Mutiny, although there was some trouble in the Ludhiana regiment. They were stationed at Benares, as were the 37th Bengal Infantry, who rebelled. In the confusion some British guns opened fire on the Ludhiana Sikhs in error. When this news reached a small Sikh detachment at Jaunpur, they mutinied and shot the adjutant. The rest of the regiment fought loyally with the British throughout the campaign, the sergeant major winning the VC.

In the reorganization of 1861 they were taken into the line as 15th (Ludhiana) Regiment Bengal Infantry. This title remained unaltered, except in the word order, until 'Bengal' was dropped in 1903. Two years later the facing colour changed from green to emerald-green (see plate 36). In 1922 they became the 2/11th Sikh regiment, the Ferozepore regiment being the 1st Battalion.

The jacket of the native officer with a wide-facing stripe was introduced in the 1880s. It is an interesting example of the survival of a military fashion. It was known as the 'Zouave' style, having been worn by the French Zouave troops whom the British had admired in the Crimea in 1854–5. The Ferozepore adopted it twenty years after that war and the Ludhiana Sikhs ten years later still.

In the pugri the native officers wore a badge of a silver circlet with XV in the centre. Other ranks had instead a large silver 'quoit', which encircled their red and yellow Sikh-style turban.

PLATE 23
40th (Pathan) Regiment Bengal Infantry (1895)

This regiment were raised as an emergency unit in 1858 as the Shahjahanpore Levy. Their various titles have been outlined on p. 22. After the Mutiny they wore red with white facings but when they became a Baluch unit they changed to drab uniform with green facings and the characteristic red trousers. These last were abandoned when they became a Pathan unit and the regiment were dressed in drab from head to foot.

Bagpipes are popular in hilly countries in many parts of the world and it was to be expected that a Pathan unit would take eagerly to a pipe band. Most Indian army units, however, adopted a Scottish plaid for their pipers. Sometimes it was a tartan to which their colonel was entitled, sometimes it was the tartan of the Scottish regiment which had trained the Indian pipers or one with which the Indian regiment had been closely associated. The 40th Pathans did not have a plaid. They used instead a style of lungi from the Kohat area. Thus the military use of the lungi, which had started as a waist sash and was then used as a rather loose turban, found yet another use, thrown over a piper's shoulder and secured with a very Scottish-looking regimental badge.

PLATE 24
19th (Punjab) Bengal Native Infantry
(1897)

One of the main factors that enabled the British and loyal Indian troops to put down the Mutiny of 1857 was the energy of John Lawrence, Chief Commissioner for the Punjab. As soon as the extent of the outbreak was realized he sent all the troops who could possibly be spared from the Punjab Irregular Force towards Delhi and set about recruiting more. Between June and December he raised seventeen battalions of infantry and two of pioneers. They all played vital roles either in the campaigns against the rebels or in keeping the peace on the North-West Frontier, which was in a particularly explosive state as the news of British reverses spread. The senior of these battalions, then known as 7th Punjab Infantry, were raised at Phillaur on the basis of a cadre from 2nd Punjab Infantry, PIF and the Punjab police.

They were taken into the regular Bengal line in 1861 and, after the change due to the remustering of the Gurkha units, became 19th (Punjab) Regiment, Bengal Infantry. In 1922 they became the senior battalion of 14th Punjab Regiment, the older Punjab battalions having become 13th Frontier Force Rifles.

The uniform, at least from 1870, was red with dark-blue facings and gold lace. The subadar in the plate, probably modelled on an officer who came to England for the diamond jubilee, wears the Zouave-type jacket then becoming rather old-fashioned even in the Indian Army.

PLATE 25
13th (Shekhawati) Bengal Native Infantry (1897)

The Shekhawati Regiment were raised in 1835 as part of the Jaipur contingent and were taken into the Company's service as a local battalion eight years later. They fought with distinction at Aliwal under Harry Smith in 1846. Remaining loyal during the Mutiny, they were taken into the Bengal line as the 13th Regiment, the Shekhawati distinction being restored in 1884. They retained it subsequently through the reforms of 1903 and 1922, in which they became 13th Rajputs and 10/16th Rajputana Rifles respectively.

Between 1856 and 1922 (when they changed to rifle green) their uniform was red with blue facings, the blue becoming darker in 1870. Their lace was gold.

PLATE 26
16th (The Lucknow Regiment) Bengal Native Infantry
(1898)

Three battalions of Bengal infantry, the 13th, 48th and 71st, mutinied at Lucknow in 1857. Enough sepoys remained loyal from these units to be formed into an improvised battalion, which fought alongside the 32nd (The Cornwall) Foot in the long defence of the Residency. In 1861 this unit was made the 16th Bengal Infantry, the title 'The Lucknow Regiment' being interpolated three years later.

In commemoration of their steadfastness they were granted a badge depicting the Baillie Gate of the Residency. This they retained when they were renamed 16th Rajputs (The Lucknow Regiment) in 1903. Their uniform was red with white facings and gold lace from 1861 until they became 10/7th Rajputs in 1922.

PLATE 27
35th (Sikh) Regiment Bengal Infantry
(1900)

After the Mutiny the number 35 was eventually awarded to the unit that had previously been the Mynpoorie Levy, but they were disbanded in 1882 as part of the economies following the fairly successful conclusion of the Second Afghan War. Five years later, on one of the recurrent scares of a Russian invasion, 5 new Bengal battalions were raised, 3 of Sikhs, one of Dogras and one of Garwhalis. The second of the Sikh battalions took the number 35 and adopted a red uniform with yellow facings and gold lace.

There are many similarities between this picture and one by A. C. Lovett, dated 1908. The main difference is that while Chater's officer wears only one medal, the Indian General Service Medal (IGS) with a single clasp, Lovett's figure has four. One of these is the India General Service Medal with one bar, while the others refer to campaigns after 1900. While Chater avoided giving his subject medals later than the date of his picture he does seem to have followed Lovett in another error. The 35th Sikhs took part in the Malakand expedition of 1897 but this would have entitled them to the India Medal 1895–1902 rather than the Indian General Service Medal. Both ribbons have a red ground with two stripes on it, the stripes for the India Medal being dark-green while those of the IGS are dark-blue. There is no doubt that the stripes in both pictures are blue and it seems very likely that Chater followed Lovett's mistake.

Central India Horse, 1893.

3rd Punjab Cavalry, 1890.

PART II
UNIFORMS AND SOLDIERS

In any army, in any century, the way in which a soldier is dressed is determined by the interaction of four factors – Economy, Impressiveness, Recognizability and Utility. These four factors strive constantly for supremacy. Sometimes one, or a combination of two or three, achieves a clear lead; sometimes others overtake them. Active service tends to simplify uniforms while a prolonged peace makes for elaboration. Changes in the capabilities of weapons impose new tactical demands, which in turn influence the kind of uniform that is desirable. The Treasury demands that changes should be few and that what changes there are must be towards simplification and cheapness. The need to secure recruits demands that uniforms must be attractive. Fashions in uniform do not change with the rapidity of those in womens' clothes but fashion is still an influence. All armies tend to change their uniform to conform with those of the army that was most recently successful. No soldier will fight the better for feeling that he looks old-fashioned.

An example of the interaction of the four factors may be found in the way the headdress of the British infantry has changed since the beginning of the nineteenth century. In 1800 the cocked hat was abandoned in favour of a tall cylindrical shako made of japanned leather with a peak to shade the eyes. Its advantages were that it was rainproof and hard-wearing, added greatly to the soldier's apparent height and provided space to display cap badges, which were then coming into fashion. Its drawbacks were that it was very heavy, was trying to wear in a high wind and was comparatively expensive. Twelve years later a modified version, known subsequently as the 'Waterloo' shako, was introduced. It was modelled on a design used in the Austrian Army, not because that army were notably successful but because they would have been Britain's allies had it not been for the unfortunate affair at Wagram. Their shako at least had the merit that it was easily distinguishable from that worn by the French. It was lighter than the 1800 model, being constructed of felt and lower in the crown. So that Impressiveness should not suffer it was equipped with a false front, which made it as tall as its predecessor. It was cheaper but not so hard-wearing and the felt was liable to get sodden in heavy rain, thus making it heavier than the old version.

It might have been thought that after Waterloo the British would have felt sufficient confidence in their own prowess to expect Europe to copy their military fashion. In fact a new design was sanctioned within two months of the battle. It was known as the 'Prussian' shako as a compliment to Blücher's army but there was no concealing the fact that the Prussians had copied it from the model worn by Napoleon's army when they were at the zenith of their fame. This apparent reaction against the trend to copy the fashions of successful armies was, in fact, a success for an alliance of Economy and Utility against Impressiveness and Recognizability. The new hat was longer lasting and weatherproof. On the other hand it was not so tall as the Waterloo shako and thus sacrificed Impressiveness, although this was to some extent compensated for by long feathers in the top. The real sacrifice was in Recognizability. The 'Prussian' model was bell-topped, being wider at the crown than at the headband, and was adopted in direct opposition to the advice of the Duke of Wellington, who had written that 'the narrow topped caps [i.e. shakos] of our infantry as opposed to the French broad topped caps, are a great advantage to those who have to look at a long line of posts opposed to each other'.

The bell-topped shako remained in use, with various modifications (including the 'Albert' shako, which succeeded in being bell-shaped while looking straight-sided), until the eve of the Crimean War. By that time the French, after Magenta and Solferino, were unquestionably the top army. Following their lead the British adopted a *képi*. This sacrificed Impressiveness almost entirely, being a rather squat peaked cap that sloped away at the back. As a utility headwear it had many advantages but, in a useless effect at Impressiveness, the British model was constructed largely of black velvet and, being shoddily made (Economy), contributed greatly to the misery of the troops wintering above Balaklava. A stouter model was issued in 1861.

French military fashions received a sharp setback in the Franco-Prussian War. At Sedan the *pickelhaube* routed the *képi*. In the mid-seventies the British infantry was issued with a modified *pickelhaube*, a cloth-covered helmet topped with a spike. This was done despite the protests of the Queen, who was 'not anxious to see the British army too much assimilated to the German. She wishes particularly to do away if possible with the spike at the top of the helmet, which Her Majesty considers neither ornamental nor useful.'

1st (Prince Albert Victor's Own) Punjab Cavalry, 1896.

The modified *pickelhaube* was the last full-dress cap worn by the infantry of the line and persisted until 1914.* It was not beautiful and was less impressive than the modification now worn by the police in the City of London. It was reasonably hard-wearing and had Economy on its side because it could be used, with a white cover, as a full-dress hat for ceremonial occasions in tropical climates.

During the lifetime of the British *pickelhaube* the British were forced to consider the fact that the soldier must have two presentable caps,† one for ceremony and the other for fighting. The troops had gone to the South African War wearing spiked helmets with covers. They had returned wearing a weird assortment devised on the spot and with a firm conviction that the helmet would not do for war. There was a move to adopt the slouch hat of the Boers, as was actually done by the armies of Australia and New Zealand. This was turned down on the

---

* It must be remembered that there were deviations in headdress for sub-species of British Infantry such as Highlanders, Lowlanders, Fusiliers and Riflemen.

† For at least a century soldiers had had a fatigue cap of more or less disreputable design but it was never worn in public. Up to 1900 the same hat did for ceremonial and fighting, except in tropical climates when the sola topi (Woseley helmet) was worn in action.

grounds that it lacked Impressiveness. Instead the civilian side of the War Office produced a version of a sailor's cap in red and blue which was known after the then Secretary of War, 'a very industrious and high-minded' politician, as the Brodrick cap. This was the most unfortunate of all British military headdresses, although it had the single virtue of cheapness. The soldiers could hardly be induced to wear it and its effect on recruiting was disastrous. It was replaced by a heavily stiffened khaki cap and it was with this that the army went to war in 1914.

The evolution of the khaki cap was directly due to the introduction of the long-range rifle, which made helmets dangerous on the battle-field. The cap, in its turn, had to be modified to cope with new, and not-so-new, weapons. At an early stage in the war of 1914 it became clear that the circular plan of the cap made it embarrassingly visible to the new-fangled flying machines. This was countered by removing the stiffening round the brim, leaving the cap more or less floppy.

The problem of visibility from the air was quickly dealt with but there was another, older, menace that also had to be circumvented. Major Henry Shrapnell's 'spherical case shot' had been adopted by the British in 1803; it was first used in action at Surinam in 1804. In 1915 it was belatedly realized by all the combatants that since shrapnel burst in the air it was likely to inflict head injuries on the troops below. The steel helmet was immediately introduced, the combatants producing a design that reflected their national attitude to their own army. The British issued an upturned steel basin that was cheap to produce and reasonably effective. The Germans introduced a scientifically designed helmet, difficult and expensive to manufacture, but shielding the vulnerable back of the neck. The French came up with an ineffective *casque*, inspired by some dim historical memory.

It was never supposed that the helmet would be worn except in times of actual or apprehended danger. At other times it could be attached to the haversack or looped on to the shoulder-strap. The serious problem was what to do with the peaked cap while the helmet was being worn. The only means of securing it to the soldier's person was a leather chin-strap which, being largely ornamental, was quite inadequate to the task. Even with all the stiffening removed it was difficult and deleterious to stuff it into the haversack.

Between the two world wars the British did their active service almost entirely in the sola topi, so the designers had plenty of time to think about a new operational hat. They started by restoring almost all the stiffening from the peaked cap, thus ensuring that it could have no active service use but was acceptable for ceremonial use when, as became usual, khaki was worn on parade. In the mid-thirties a khaki deerstalker was suggested but found no favour. At the time of the Munich crisis the designers produced their final answer, a hat almost as disastrous as the Brodrick cap.

The 'cap, field service' of 1938 consisted of a much-modified forage cap and had the twin advantages of being the cheapest hat ever produced and of being so thin when not in use that it took up no more space in the haversack than a folded newspaper. On the other hand it was strikingly unimpressive; it afforded no shelter from sun or rain; it was too inconspicuous to be blown off by a high wind, but would fall off if the soldier turned his head smartly. There was clearly little to be said for a hat that had no virtues except when it was not being worn. The obvious alternative was the beret, which had been worn by armoured troops since 1916. Economy, however, had another attempt at influencing the inevitable and, on the grounds that berets required rare skills in manufacture, the long-suffering soldier was issued with a 'cap, general service', a hybrid shaped rather like a beret but made (by what appeared to be highly unskilled labour) from strips of khaki cloth. By the end of the war the beret had replaced it.

Having seen how four factors – Economy, Impressiveness, Recognizability and Utility – have affected one item of military clothing in one branch of one army, we must now look more closely at the factors individually. Economy, as has been seen, usually succeeds in defeating its own ends in military affairs. How it started off belatedly in the matter of British (and to some extent Indian) uniforms is a case in point. The European tradition was that the business of raising an army was a matter for private enterprise. If a government wished to recruit an army directly it must create an elaborate and expensive organization to do so. No British parliament before the Crimean War would have sanctioned either the expenditure or the creation of the necessary jobs in the gift of government. Even if such an organization had been sanctioned the officers and soldiers (or possibly civil servants) who staffed it would be, at best, second-rate. It would be a trying service and one that would offer greater job security if it were done slowly. If a mass of recruits was raised quickly the recruiters would be redundant. It was cheaper to farm the whole business out to the colonels of regiments who needed recruits. No regimental soldier liked touting for recruits and they could be counted on to get the business over as quickly as possible. From the Treasury's point of view the most economical way of setting about it was to pay a lump sum for every recruit. Some of this was paid over to the recruit in the form of a bounty, some provided for his uniform and necessaries. The balance represented profit for the recruiters. A proportion of this went to the colonel of the regiment, some to the captain of the recruit's company. The recruiting party, headed by a subaltern or sergeant, divided the balance in shares graded according to rank. Any disbursements, mostly in the form of liquid gratuities to likely recruits, came out of the profit and did not have to be accounted for to the Treasury. The system also introduced a measure of competition into the operation, since many regiments were competing for the available pool of recruits. Thus the government secured the maximum of soldiers while expanding a minimum of money and effort.

The corollary was that the business of providing uniforms for a regiment fell, subject to certain checks on quality, into the hands of the colonel. Each year a lump sum was paid into his account from which he was expected to clothe his regiment (and which, in the meantime, he could invest or use as he thought best). The underlying theory was that the colonel would be anxious to economize on the issue of uniform so as to increase his own profit. In practice this was seldom the case. After about 1800, when colonelcies stopped being given for political services and were used as a reward for distinguished or deserving soldiers, the aim of almost every colonel was to increase the efficiency and prestige of his regiment (which in itself made recruiting easier and more profitable). Since the colonel was responsible for clothing his regiment, he naturally assumed that he could, within generous limits, clothe it as he fancied. All introduced minor regimental distinctions; some spent vast sums of their own money on embellishing their men.

When the government eventually took over responsibility for providing uniforms directly, they found themselves faced with a plenitude of minute variations, all of which cost money to provide and all of which, they were assured, were essential to the well-being and fighting quality of the troops. They made determined attempts at standardization but seldom achieved any lasting successes. It was difficult for them to know where to draw the line. The 28th Foot were authorized by Royal Warrant to wear their regimental number on the back of their shakos to commemorate their gallantry at Alexandria. The cost of this distinction was small, a penny or two a man, but it fell on the colonel, who had to pay it out of his lump sum. When, fifty years after, the government took over the supply of uniforms they could scarcely refuse to pay a little more for the back-badge of the North Gloucesters. But what were they to do with the embellishments of the 17th Lancers, on whom their colonel had spent so much of his

6th Jat Light Infantry, 1903.

own money that they were known as 'Bingham's Dandies'? The Treasury is still paying for distinctions that would never have arisen if colonels had not been given charge of regimental clothing as an eighteenth-century economy.

Many of the same considerations applied in India. The regular units of the Company's armies were not raised with colonels as proprietors but the irregular regiments were formed on a very similar basis, except that there was no hope of their commander making a profit. A promising young officer was told to go to an area and raise a unit. Sometimes he was given a lump sum to launch the regiment. In other cases, as with Lumsden and the Guides, he had to find the money as best he could. The question of how his officers and men were to be dressed (and armed) was left to the commanders' discretion. They left behind them a legacy of peculiarities of dress that eventually became a charge to the government of India, the more so since, in Bengal, the army was rebuilt after the Mutiny on a basis of the irregular regiments. It is, incidentally, interesting to speculate that the peculiarities in dress of the irregular troops may have been a factor in maintaining their loyalty when the 'uniformly' clad regular mutinied. It might be possible to compute the cost to the Indian Government of supplying yellow cloth to Skinner's Horse between 1861 (when they became a regular regiment) and 1922 (when their distinctive full dress was officially abolished).

Impressiveness is a prime function of a uniform and operates in three ways – on the enemy, on the onlooker, on the wearer. In the days when battles were fought face to face it was of vital importance that a soldier should look as imposing as could be contrived. The easiest way of achieving this was by giving him a tall headdress. Even savages, whose 'uniform' consisted of an exiguous loincloth, wore feathers on their heads to increase their apparent height. This practice is continued in the feathered bonnets of highland regiments and the nodding plumes of cavalrymen. In its extreme form it is represented by the bearskin caps of the Foot Guards.

There were other ways of making a man look fearsome apart from giving him imposing hats. His apparent height could also be increased by making him wear white cross-belts on his chest. They constricted his movements, were almost impossible to keep clean on service and the point where they crossed made a convenient aiming mark for a sharpshooter but, with ranges short and muskets inaccurate, this latter point was an acceptable hazard. Strips of lace or braiding across the chest made the shoulders appear broader and brawnier and the same effect could be increased by adding large epaulettes with conspicuous fringes. With the use of such aids, soldiers of normal size could be made to seem giants. The effect could, however, be overdone and in some of Rowlandson's cartoons small men in bearskins and wide epaulettes appear as figures of fun.

To impress an onlooker was, at bottom, an attempt to prevent him from becoming an enemy. Any potentate seems more powerful when surrounded by a glittering retinue of aides and guards. In any army the Sovereign's bodyguard are the most imposing in their size and uniform. Even Marxist republics feel it worthwhile maintaining guard divisions and in France the *Garde Républicaine* retains much of the glamour of the Imperial Guards of the two Napoleons. Household troops are, in fact, an early form of public relations. Their purpose is to impress and their uniforms are designed for splendour rather than utility. The body armour of the British Household Cavalry was introduced entirely for show at the time of the coronation of George IV. They have never had to fight in it.

In India the Governor General and the two (later three) Governors all kept bodyguards with largely ceremonial functions. Although two of the bodies had earned battle honours, their main purpose was to reflect imperial glory. India, however, was a special case. The subcontinent teemed with potentates. As late as 1946 there were still 567 independent princes within the Indian Empire and every one of them was capable of making a superb appearance with a glittering escort. It was therefore essential that the British officials who dealt with them should be able to put on a grand show. Any of the Indian cavalry regiments might be called upon to form part of a pageant designed to impress.

To the soldier a splendid uniform was an incentive to enlist and an encouragement to steadiness after he had enlisted. Few nineteenth-century uniforms made many concessions to comfort but they unquestionably stood out in a crowd. A soldier might have to merge his personality in his regiment but when out of barracks he could feel that his uniform gave him an individuality denied to his fellow men. There were few civilians who did not secretly envy the soldier his uniform, however much they might affect to despise soldiering as a profession. It was that most unmilitary of figures, Samuel Johnson, who declared: 'Every man thinks meanly of himself for not having been a soldier, or not having been at sea.' Dr Johnson's theoretical preference would seem to have been for the army, since he remarked that 'no man will be a sailor who has the contrivance to get himself into jail'.

A uniform that was distinctive could serve quite as well as one that was glamourous. Most men prefer working as one of a team. 'Patriotism,' as was remarked in another context, 'is not enough.' A man needs some smaller, more identifiable group within which to work and to which he can devote his loyalty. This loyalty he could focus on his regiment. The business of focusing was made easier by distinctions of dress that singled him out from other soldiers. The dress did not have to be glamorous. Lumsden's Guides in their 'drab' were probably the plainest dressed soldiers in the world but the uniqueness of their uniform helped to produce recruits in embarrassingly large numbers. Half a century earlier the beribboned recruiting sergeants of the redcoat regiments could offer no inducements to compete with the sombre green and black of Coote Manningham's Riflemen.

Recognizability was a virtue that became a vice. Until the middle of the nineteenth century battles were fought with muskets that were not accurate at 100 yards and even artillery could inflict crippling casualties only up to 300 yards from the muzzle; the maximum effective range of case shot was 300 yards; round shot, which could carry 1,000 yards and more, could inflict heavy casualties only on troops in close formation. Muskets and cannon alike emitted dense

7th Bombay Lancers (Baluch Horse), 1900.

clouds of black smoke. Action was joined in a thick fog. There was no better form of communication than a man on a horse with a verbal message. Generalship depended on being able to see which troops were one's own and which were the enemy's. Bright and distinctive colours were as essential for the opposing armies as they are now for the teams in a football match. From the soldier's point of view a bright colour was as effective as any other. There was no advantage in camouflaging clothing when two bodies of troops were battering at each other at a range of 50 yards with every man standing up, since it was impossible to load the musket lying down. The soldier's chief concern, as usual, was that he should not be shot at by his own side.

Conditions changed from the middle of the century. The introduction of the rifle as the normal weapon for the infantryman meant that the fire-fight was conducted at ever-increasing ranges. The British in the Crimea were using a rifle that was effective at more than 500 yards. At Omdurman forty years later the Guards Brigade opened fire at 2,700 yards. By that time black powder was a thing of the past and smokeless propellants meant that there was clear visibility on the battlefield so that, very soon, ways of laying smoke had to be invented. It was clear that Recognizability would have to take a back seat. British troops last fought wearing scarlet in 1885. The last Indian cavalry regiment went on active service wearing blue as late as 1895 (see notes, plate 9). In continental Europe the lesson took longer to learn: in 1914 French infantry were still wearing blue jackets and scarlet trousers.

It was in India that the death knell of Recognizability was sounded. When Harry Lumsden founded the Guides, the Commissioner in the Punjab, Henry Lawrence, laid down that 'to get the best work out of the troops, and to enable them to undertake great exertions, it was necessary for them to be loosely, comfortably and suitably clad'. Lumsden, who had 'the arming and dressing according to my own fancy', made some experiments in using native dress for them but found that this made it too difficult to tell friend from foe even at short ranges. He therefore decided to dress them uniformly in a mud colour. Each man was issued with a long smock, baggy trousers and a cotton turban made of home-spun cotton and dyed with mazari, a dye produced from an indigenous dwarf palm, to a drab grey colour. Since, however, much of the Guides' work was done in the mountains, they were also issued with sheepskin jackets. Mazari failed to dye these satisfactorily and instead they were treated with mulberry juice, which gave them a yellow drab, authentically mud-coloured effect that was known as khaki, from the Urdu *khak* meaning dust. The Guides continued to dye their own uniforms until 1904.

The example of the Guides was followed by 5 of the first 6 battalions of Punjab infantry raised in 1849. The other battalion, the 1st (later known as Coke's Rifles), wore rifle green. Khaki did not spread to the rest of the army, British or Indian, until the Mutiny, when the appearance of the Punjab troops in the Bengal presidency inspired many British units, led by the 52nd Light Infantry, to improvise a dye for their white tropical uniforms.

As soon as the suppression of the Mutiny was complete, the use of khaki, except by the PIF, was forbidden. It was reintroduced for service wear in 1861, only to be suppressed again three years later. It was, however, in general use among Indian units at the beginning of the Second Afghan War in 1879, although the British 17th Foot had hurriedly to dye their whites with river mud before starting on the campaign. In 1881 khaki was officially recognized as being the colour for the service dress of British and Indian troops in India and the British adopted another shade for use in Africa soon afterwards. It was not until 1902, after they had experimented with grey tweed uniforms, that the British decided that service uniforms for all parts of the world should be khaki or, as it was described officially 'drab mixture'.

The consideration of Utility in uniforms has been left to the last. It is sometimes tempting to think that the same was the case when some uniforms were designed. It is difficult to come to any other conclusion when considering the leather stock that was introduced for British troops in about 1800. Its purpose was to force the soldier to keep his head upright (Impressiveness) and to replace the two neck-cloths with which he was previously issued (Economy). It was scarcely a contribution to Utility since it made it very difficult for him to bend his head down far enough to sight along the barrel of his musket. It was nevertheless retained for several decades.

Yet there are certain irreducible demands for Utility that cannot be overlooked in designing any military dress. The seams of the fighting soldier's jacket must not be drawn so tight that he cannot handle his musket. He must have a pouch in which to store his ammunition and a haversack in which he can carry the basic minimum of rations, some cleaning materials, a spare shirt and a pair of socks. All this is easier for the cavalryman who has a horse to carry the weight and keep his finery out of the mud. The infantryman, on the other hand, must be allowed enough room in his breeches to be able to march long distances and to have serviceable boots. It may be that one of the reasons why Britain lost her American colonies was that her infantrymen were supplied with long gaiters, buttoning to the knee, which took twelve minutes to put on. Similarly it was not until 1847 that the advocates of Economy relented suffciently to allow the infantryman to have boots that were designed separately to fit left and right feet.

The influence of Utility is in direct relationship to the amount of active service an army has undertaken in the immediate past. A prolonged peace gives a licence to the tailors and lace merchants. War gives Utility its head. It was in the years of Sir Garnet Wolseley's greatest influence that the British adopted a service dress instead of fighting in their ceremonial wear. As a young officer Wolseley could remember struggling through the steamy jungles of Burma in a high-collared scarlet jacket and, according to orders, white gloves. He had also served in the Crimea, where the instructions for what was expected to be an opposed landing prescribed 'full dress without plumes'.

Fighting soldiers quickly learn to modify the uniform issued to them so as to make it as functional as possible. As long as hostilities continue deviations from the *Dress Regulations* are winked at by the senior commanders. One of Wellington's young officers wrote that 'provided we brought our men into the field well appointed with their sixty rounds of ammunition, he never looked to see whether their trousers were black, blue or grey'. Wellington himself thought it 'indifferent how a soldier is clothed, provided it is in a uniform manner; and that he is forced to keep himself clean'.

The testing time comes when the war is over. Then field commanders, however successful, cease to have any pre-eminent influence on what the army wears. We have already seen how, eight weeks after Waterloo, the British adopted a shako in direct opposition to Wellington's wishes. The Duke is usually said to have been supreme in military matters until his death in 1852 but, when it came to uniform, he was no match for George IV and William IV, both of whom took a keen, almost obsessive interest in military dress. George IV succeeded in dressing his Household Cavalry in a helmet so imposing that it would carry a man off his horse in a high wind. Wellington certainly disapproved of this folly but he could not resist it and, as colonel of the Royal Horse Guards, he must have had to pay to supply them for his regiment.

One notable contribution to Utility, apart from khaki, emerged from the Indian Army. In 1849 a young lieutenant raised the 2nd Regiment of Punjab cavalry. Nine years later, at Sirpura, he and a single sowar charged and captured a rebel cannon. He won the Victoria Cross but lost his left arm. Despite his disability he continued in the army until he became a general in 1888. He took part in several campaigns on the frontier and while he found no trouble handling his sword and pistol he experienced difficulty in securing them when not in use. In particular he was anxious to have his holster so arranged that if his pistol went off accidentally, as was not uncommon in the days before the safety catch, it would not hit any part of his person. With this in mind he designed a leather belt with a shoulder-brace, which is still worn in many armies and police forces. In 1904 the regiment he had raised fifty-five years earlier was officially retitled Sam Browne's Cavalry.

1903–22
(CAVALRY)

PLATE 28
18th Tiwana Lancers
(1903)

Although no race in India had taken longer to be subdued by the British than the Mahrattas, two regiments of Mahratta cavalry were raised in 1858 when the British were in dire trouble and both fought loyally during the Mutiny campaigns. The 2nd Mahratta Horse was joined in its early months by a squadron of Tiwanas, Rajputs from the Jhelum valley, south of Rawalpindi.

While the 1st Mahratta Horse were disbanded in 1860, the 2nd Regiment became the 18th Bengal Cavalry in the following year and were converted to lancers in 1885. When the presidency titles were abolished in 1903 the regiment became 18th Tiwana Lancers. Three years later when the Prince of Wales visited India they became 'Prince of Wales's Own' and when the Prince succeeded to the throne the title was altered to 18th King George's Own Lancers. The regiment provided the escort for George v when he made his state entry into Delhi in 1912.

The full-dress uniform was scarlet with blue facings and gold lace. A plain blue kummerbund was worn in field service order.

PLATE 29
1st Duke of York's Own Lancers
(Skinner's Horse)
(1910)

James Skinner was the son of a British officer and an Indian lady of rank. He saw his first action as a mercenary officer in the service of the Mahrattas. When war between his Indian masters and the British became imminent he was released from his engagements and took service with the British. In 1803 he raised a regiment of local horse dressed in yellow, which served with distinction under Lord Lake. He armed them with lances and tulwars (curved broad swords) since he did not believe that Indian cavalrymen could be proficient with the sabre.

They continued as local horse until 1840 when, during the First Afghan War, it was found that they were not entitled to draw rations from the commissariat. Shortly before the men and horses were disabled by starvation they were reclassified as 1st Bengal Irregular Cavalry, whereupon the commissariat consented to issue rations.

The defection of the whole Bengal cavalry of the line during the Mutiny meant that Skinner's, as the senior irregular regiment, became 1st Bengal Cavalry and were armed with the sabre. They retained their yellow uniforms but had red facings until 1895, when they became lancers once more and changed to black facings and kummer-bunds. The suffix 'Skinner's Horse' was officially recognized in 1901.

The colour of the kurta in this plate is more ochre in tone than the example in the Indian Army room at Sandhurst but there is plenty of evidence that this shade was actually worn at times.

PLATE 30
3rd Skinner's Horse
(1910)

At the time of Waterloo there were 3 regiments of Skinner's Horse. The 3rd were disbanded in 1819 but the 2nd, known for a time as Baddeley's Horse, survived and became 3rd Bengal Cavalry after the Mutiny. When the Bengal title was dropped in 1903 the official title for 2nd Skinner's Horse became 3rd Skinner's Horse. The two regiments were reunited in 1922 as 1st Duke of York's Own Skinner's Horse.

The 2nd (or 3rd) regiment retained the yellow uniform until 1870, when they began a series of changes. They adopted red in that year, drab in 1881 and blue with yellow facings in 1891. Unlike the 1st Regiment they retained the distinctive lance pennon in blue and yellow. Every other Indian lancer regiment (except 19th Bengal Lancers [Fane's Horse], which kept blue and white) changed their pennon colours to the traditional red and white of Poland.

Chater dated this plate 1903 but the source material was undoubtedly Lovett's picture of 1910.

PLATE 31
21st Prince Albert Victor's Own Cavalry (Frontier Force) (Daly's Horse) (1911)

Five regiments of Punjab cavalry were raised in 1849 and 4 of them survived until 1922. The other one, the 4th, was broken up in 1882 at a time when 4 Indian cavalry regiments were disbanded in order to provide an extra squadron for the remainder. The senior of these regiments was 1st Cavalry, Punjab Frontier Force. They were entitled Prince Albert Victor's Own in honour of the Duke of Clarence, eldest son of King Edward VII, then Prince of Wales.

From the time of the Mutiny the regiment wore a dark-blue uniform. The lace was silver until 1868, when it changed to gold. In that year the facings were red but they changed to scarlet in 1905.

The suffix 'Daly's Horse' was authorized in 1904 to commemorate Lieutenant Henry Daly, formerly second-in-command to Lumsden in the Guides, who raised the regiment at Lahore.

Although the artist calls the regiment Daly's Horse he dates the picture 1901. It would seem nevertheless that the source material was from some years later since the officer depicted appears to be wearing the Indian General Service Medal, which was first issued in 1908. The clasp worn on it would be that for North-West Frontier 1908, a bar to which the 21st were entitled.

PLATES 32
Governor General's Bodyguard
(1912)

The Governor's Bodyguard in Bengal is the longest surviving unit of Indian Cavalry. It was founded in 1773 and was known as the Governor's Troop of Mughals. Although its duties were largely ceremonial, being concerned with guarding and escorting the Governor (later Governor General), the unit saw some active service and was awarded battle honours for *Java* and *Ava* beside four for the Sikh wars. The Governor General did not go on these campaigns. The last Governor General to contemplate taking the field was the Marquess of Wellesley who proposed accompanying the Commander-in-Chief, Madras in the campaign against Seringapatam in 1799. He was dissuaded by his younger brother Arthur, then a colonel, who wrote with his usual forthrightness, 'Your presence in the camp, instead of giving confidence to the general, would in fact deprive him of the command of the army. If I were in General Harris's situation and you joined the army, I should quit it.'

Like British household troops, the Bodyguard's uniform was scarlet with blue facings. The lace was silver until they became royal troops after the Mutiny when it was changed to gold.

PLATE 33
Governor's Bodyguard, Madras
(1912)

Each of the Governors of the Presidencies had a Bodyguard, that of Madras being formed in 1778. Bombay did without ceremonial troops until 1865 and the Bodyguard for the Governor of Bengal was not raised until 1912 when the Governor General (Viceroy) and his Guard moved to New Delhi.

The Madras Guard were unusual in that they retained the alkalak after most of the cavalry had gone over to the kurta. Another curious feature was that the native officers wore, according to the *Dress Regulations* for 1885 and 1901, white moleskin breeches.

(INFANTRY)
PLATE 34
106th Hazara Pioneers
(1904)

Much of the Indian Army's work was done in roadless country and there was a steady demand for battalions of pioneers. Many were raised at various times but few of them had a long career. The usual practice was to raise them in a hurry when they were needed and disband them as soon as the immediate emergency was over. The Hazara Pioneers had a longer run than most. They were raised in 1904 and disbanded in a burst of economy in 1933. During their short life they were given the number belonging to the 6th Bombay Infantry, which had been disbanded in the economies of 1882.

The uniform was drab with red facings until 1914, at which time full dress almost ceased to be worn. Then it was changed to scarlet with plum facings.

PLATE 35
33rd Punjab Infantry
(1905)

This was the most junior of the regiments raised by Lawrence in the Punjab in 1857. They were originally known as the Allahabad Levy and were taken into the Bengal line as the 37th Native Infantry in 1861. Between 1864 and 1885 they had the subtitle 'Allahabad'. Five years later they became known as the 33rd (Punjabi Mahomedan) Regiment.

Chater dates this plate 1902 but in that year the regiment were still wearing scarlet with white facings. The drab uniform with green facings was not adopted until 1905.

PLATE 36
15th Ludhiana Sikhs
(1908)

The outline of the career of this regiment has been given in the note on plate 22. The principal change in the uniform is the abandonment of the Zouave jacket with its panels of the facing colour in favour of a plainer type approximating to the contemporary British style.

The officer depicted wears among other decorations the Order of British India, 1st Class, the medal for Egypt (1882–9), with the clasp for Suakim, the Khedival Star for the same campaign and the India Medal 1895–1902. The four bars on this would be Relief of Chitral, Punjab Frontier 1897–8, Samana 1897 and Tirah, all of which were awarded to the 15th Sikhs.

PLATE 37
14th (King George's Own) Ferozepore Sikhs (1913)

The 14th Sikhs were the companion regiment to the Ludhiana Regiment (see notes on plate 22) and were raised at Ferozepore in 1846. They were taken into the line as 14th Bengal Infantry in 1861, the title Ferozepore being added three years later. They became Prince of Wales's Own when the Prince visited India in 1906 and King George's Own when he succeeded to the throne.

In 1913 the Ferozepores provided one of the King's Indian orderly officers in Britain and it is probable that it was from a photograph of that officer that Chater obtained his source material.

PLATE 38
69th Punjabis
(1913)

As their number in the sixties indicates, they were originally a Madras regiment, being raised in 1764 as the 10th Coast Sepoys. They were renamed in turn 10th Carnatic Regiment, 9th Carnatic Regiment and 9th Madras Native Infantry. In the reorganization of 1903 it was officially recognized that they had very little connection with Madras or the Carnatic and they were renamed 69th Punjabis.

From 1801 the regiment's facings were always green, but the shade was varied. Until 1882 it was gosling-green; then it changed to dark-green (1882) and emerald (1891). In 1922 they became the 2/2nd Punjabis and the facings became grass-green.

1922–39

The reorganization of 1922 cut heavily into the number of Indian cavalry regiments. Apart from the bodyguards there had been 39 of them. They were now reduced to 21. None was disbanded but only three, the Guides and the 27th and 28th Light Cavalry, escaped amalgamation. All regiments changed their number except the 1st (Skinner's Horse) and the 2nd (Gardner's Horse).

At the same time a wholesale simplification of full-dress uniform was decreed. In future every regiment would wear blue, and facing colours were to be accorded to groups of regiments. Thus 1st to 3rd would have primrose facings, 4th to 6th and 13th to 15th scarlet, 7th to 9th and 16th to 18th French-grey and 10th to 12th and 19th to 21st blue. This reform coincided with the virtual abolition of full dress. Very few officers wore it unless they were on duty at Viceregal Lodge or were selected to do a tour as King's Indian orderly officer at Buckingham Palace. Although a few officers acquired the new-style uniform, most used the pre-1922 uniform of their regiments, with or without minor gestures towards the new regulations.

PLATE 39
16th Light Cavalry
(1934)

This regiment was the old 2nd Madras Lancers (see plates 10 and 16), later the 27th Light Cavalry. The post-1922 uniform should have been dark-blue with French-grey facings. Instead the orderly officer who came to England in 1934 wore the old uniform of the regiment, except that he had the girdle of a British lancer officer instead of a kummerbund.

PLATE 40
2nd Lancers (Gardner's Horse) (1934)

Gardner's Horse retained their number in the 1922 renumbering, since the 3rd (Skinner's Horse) naturally rejoined their senior unit as the 1st Regiment. Gardner's therefore amalgamated with the 4th Cavalry.

William Gardner raised the regiment in 1809 and until 1870 (by which time it was 2nd Bengal Cavalry) the uniform was green with red trousers (pyjamas). It was followed by a blue uniform with light-blue facings.

The 4th Cavalry were raised in 1838 as the cavalry element of the forces supplied by the semi-independent state of Oudh. They became 6th Bengal Irregular Cavalry two years later and 4th (regular) Bengal Cavalry after the Mutiny. At that stage they had a red uniform with blue facings.

The authorized uniform for the combined unit was blue with primrose facings but in the late twenties a dispensation was obtained allowing them to revert to the light-blue facings of Gardner's Horse.

PLATE 41
15th Lancers
(1937)

One of the most outstanding figures at the coronation of King George VI in 1937 was Risaldar Major Sher Khan, 15th Lancers. Like the three other Indian orderly officers he had had the ends of his pugri stiffened and arranged in a fan shape. This practice, which developed in India between the two world wars, is a late example of devices intended to increase the apparent height of the wearer.

The 15th Lancers were formed by the amalgamation of the 17th Cavalry and the 37th Lancers (Baluch Horse). Neither of the two constituent regiments was of great antiquity. The 17th had been raised in 1885, filling the place of another Bengal regiment that had been disbanded on the grounds of economy three years earlier. The reraised 17th had a blue uniform and white facings. They were the only wholly Muslim cavalry unit in the army and had as their badge the crescent and star. They had no battle honours but had a unique mounted pipe band.

Their partners, the 37th Lancers, were also raised in 1885 as the 7th Bombay Cavalry. They were given the title Baluch Horse in the following year and converted to lancers three years later. Their original uniform was green with buff facings but changed to drab in 1898.

Sher Khan's uniform at the coronation was that of the 17th Cavalry with the distinctive gold lace ornamentation across the chest. In 1922 scarlet facings were ordered but these was changed in 1928 to buff, as a concession to the 37th Lancers.

Glossary

ALKALAK (or ALKHALAK) A long coat, fastening on the chest, worn by mounted men. It was, in most cavalry regiments, superseded by the KURTA, but was retained in some regiments such as the Bodyguards. (Plates 32 and 33.)

BATTALION COMPANIES Until the second half of the nineteenth century an infantry battalion was organized with two flank companies: the Grenadiers (or assault troops), who paraded on the right of the line; and the Light Company (or skirmishers) on the left. The remainder were known as battalion (or centre) companies. Their number varied with the financial climate between four and eight.

BRINJARRIES Merchants dealing in grain and rice who, since the Indian Army had no supply system of its own (except for ammunition), travelled with the army on the march selling to the commissaries on little more than a day-to-day basis.

CHENILLE A fur or worsted crest worn on the ridge of a dragoon-style helmet.

DAFFADAR (or DUFFADAR) Sergeant of Indian cavalry.

DAK (or DAWK) The mail carried by relays of horses or camels. Travelling by post in India usually meant moving by palanquin carried by bearers from one Dak bungalow to another.

DOOLIE A litter with canopy for carrying the sick and wounded.

GHI 'Clarified butter' used in cooking.

HAVILDAR Sergeant of Indian infantry.

JAPANNED Treated with a lacquer originating in Japan which produced a shiny black surface.

JAWAN Is literally 'a youth' (as an adjective *jawan* means 'young'). It was used as a general term for at least the younger soldiers. SIPAHI ('sepoy') is the formal word for 'soldier'.

JEMADAR The junior commissioned rank in both the cavalry and infantry, roughly equivalent to cornet or ensign. To be distinguished from ZEMIDAR, a landed proprietor or tax-collector.

KEPI A cap with a flat top sloping towards the front and a horizontal peak. The word is derived from the German-Swiss *Kappi*, a little cap.

KOT-DAFFADAR, KOT-SUBADAR Senior NCO, squadron (or company) sergeant major.

KHAKI Dust-coloured (see p. 101).

KULLA (or KULLAH) A close-fitting cap, usually pointed at the top, round which the PUGRI is tied in Muslim and Jat regiments.

KUMMERBUND (or CUMMERBUND, or CUMMERBAND, or KUMMERBAND) Sash worn round the waist.

KURTA (or KURTAH) A loose-fitting frock or blouse usually opening at the front but sometimes slit at the sides. It reached to the knees. The usual wear for cavalry after the Mutiny.

LUNGI (or LUNGHI)   Originally a type of KUMMERBUND, it became used as headwear, being a loosely tied PUGRI.

MAMELUKE-HILTED   A type of hilt, derived from a Turkish model, with a simple cruciform hand-guard (frequently much decorated). Since it gave little protection to the hand it was normally worn only by general and staff officers.

NAIK (or NAIQUE)   Corporal, hence LANCE-NAIK.

PESHWA (or PESHWAR)   First, hence prime minister or chief magistrate. In practice frequently the effective ruler and paying only notional alleigiance to the titular head of state.

PICKELHAUBE   Literally a basin-bonnet with a spike. The spiked helmet worn by the German Army.

PICKERS   Steel needles, secured to the belt by chains, used to clear the touch-holes of flintlock firearms.

PUGRI (or PAGRI or PUGGREE or PUGGARI)   Cloth worn round the head to form a turban. In a smaller form it could be worn round a helmet or sola topi.

RISALLAH (or RISALA or RUSSALAH)   A body of cavalry. This could be as small as a troop or as large as a regiment or even a brigade. The only limit to its size seems to have been that it was smaller than a durrah. A durrah is defined only as a corps, a term used in the early nineteenth century for any body of men from a regiment to a group of several divisions.

RISALDAR   Indian cavalry officer equivalent to a lieutenant. Up to 1866 this was the senior rank open to Indian officers. Subsequently each regiment had one RISALDAR MAJOR, equivalent to a captain.

RYOT   Peasant or labourer.

SABRETACHE   A satchel carried on SLINGS from the belt by cavalrymen and, up to about 1830, by field officers of infantry. It was intended to contain writing materials and, although the face was usually heavily ornamented, the reverse could be used as a portable writing desk.

SEPOY (originally SIPAHI)   An Indian private soldier of infantry or artillery.

SHAKO   A rigid and usually peaked cap. The shape is either cylindrical or a truncated cone. From the Magyar *csáko süveg*, a peakèd cap.

SILLADAR   A cavalryman who provides his own horse.

SLINGS   Short straps depending from the waist-belt. For a mounted man this was the most convenient method of attaching the sword to the person but when he dismounted the weapon dragged along the ground. Although most infantry officers carried their swords in frogs, which held them close to the body, light infantry and riflemen who had the most need of mobility wore sword slings so that one hand was needed to stop the scabbard getting between their legs.

SOWAR   An Indian trooper, or private soldier in the cavalry.

SUBADAR   The infantry equivalent of a RISALDAR. After 1866 there were also SUBADARS MAJOR.

SYCE (or SICE)   Groom.

TULWAR (or TALWAR)   Curved Indian sword with a scimitar-style blade.

Source of Quotations

Sources quoted in the text.

p. 6. line 6. Roberts, Frederick, Lord. *Forty One Years in India,* 1897.
p. 6. line 18. Hart's *Quarterly Army List* for January 1847.
p. 7. line 1. Majende, V. D. *Up among the Pandies,* 1859.
p. 7. line 19. Blakiston, John. *Twelve Years Military Adventure,* 1840.
p. 13. line 41. Wellington, 1st Duke of, *Supplementary Despatches,* 1858.
p. 14. line 41. Majende, *op. cit.*
p. 17. line 4. *Selections from the Letters, Despatches and other State Papers concerning the Indian Mutiny.* (Ed. G. W. Forrest) 1893.
p. 19. line 2. Shand, Alexander Innes. *General John Jacob,* 1900.
p. 20. line 6. ib.
p. 23. line 20. Adye, John. *Recollections of a Military Life,* 1895.
p. 27. line 40. Benyon, W. G. L., *With Kelly to Chitral,* 1896.
p. 28. line 19. ib.
p. 29. line 3. Creagh, O'Moore. *Autobiography,* 1924.
p. 29. line 28. Gordon, Thomas, *A Varied Life,* 1906.
p. 30. line 22. Roberts, *op. cit.,* and Richards, Frank. *Old Soldier Sahib,* 1936.
p. 31. line 13. Steel, F. A. *The Complete Indian Housekeeper and Cook,* 1898.
p. 32, line 19. Roberts, *op. cit.*
p. 32. line 29. Creagh, *op. cit.*
p. 92. line 39. Verner, Willoughby, *Military Life of HRH the Duke of Cambridge,* 1905.
p. 102. line 41. Grattan, William, *Adventures with the Connaught Rangers,* 1847.

Other Principal Sources.

Cambridge, 2nd Marquess of. *Notes on the Armies of India,* Journal of the Society for Army Historical Research, Nos. 189–194.
Carman, W. Y. *Indian Army Uniforms – Cavalry,* 1961.
Carman, W. Y. *Indian Army Uniforms – Infantry,* 1969.
Dilks, David. *Curzon in India,* 1969.
Elliott, J. G. *The Frontier 1839–1947,* 1968.
Jackson, Donovan. *India's Armies,* 1942.
Macmunn, G. F. and Lovett, A. C. *Armies of India,* 1911.
Smith Dorrien, Horace. *Memories of Forty Eight Years Service,* 1925.
Woodruff, Philip. *The Men who ruled India,* 1954.
Younghusband, George. *Historical Records of the Queen's Own Corps of Guides,* 1886.

Index

The figures in italics refer to plate numbers

The Queen's Own Corps of Guides,
Punjab Frontier Force (Cavalry). 1900.

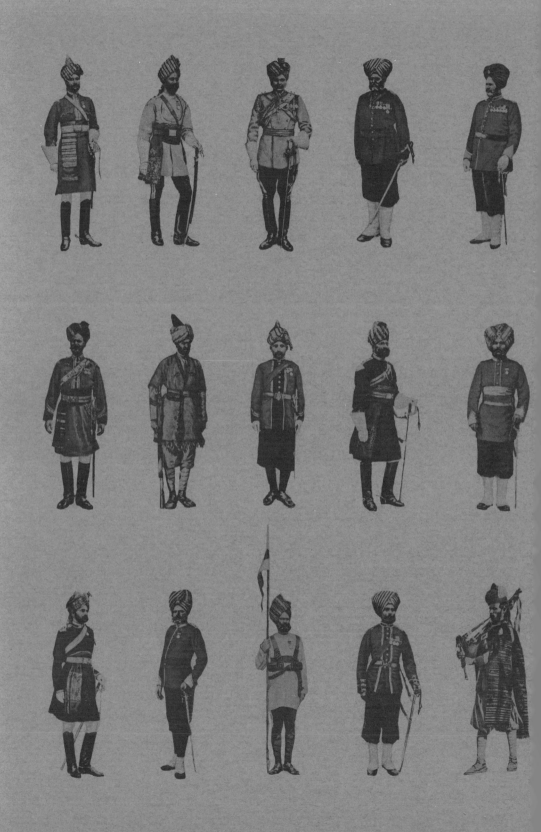